DAKSHAYANI

DR. ARUNA MUKIM

PRABHAT
PAPERBACKS

Published by

PRABHAT PAPERBACKS

An Imprint of Prabhat Prakashan Pvt. Ltd.
4/19 Asaf Ali Road,
New Delhi–110 002 (INDIA)
e-mail: prabhatbooks@gmail.com

ISBN 978-93-5521-296-2
DAKSHAYNI
by Dr. Aruna Mukim

Edition
2022

Price
₹ 250 (Rupees Two Hundred Fifty Only)

Printed at
Sanjay Printer, Sahibabad

PROLOGUE

Prajapatipati Daksha was very happy while looking fondly at his baby daughter. Looking at his wife, he asked, “Isn’t she the most beautiful child around, Prasuti?”

Flashing a smile at her husband, she just mumbled, “You speak the truth Prajapati! Even I just want to keep looking at her all the time.” She paused and, then casting a long glance at her husband, she said, “When she grows up, she’ll make you a proud father! There’s something unique about her very appearance!”

“I’ll ask Bhrigu to draw her horoscope as soon as possible. I’m very sure that her stars will be as radiant as she is! Just look at her eyes! It seems as if they carry the entire universe in them! My dear wife, we’re lucky to have a daughter with this enticing splendor!”

Prasuti then said, “I’m sure that we’ll both get along well with him.”

Suddenly, Prajapati Daksha said, “We must celebrate her coming to our family in a big way and also, we must choose a beautiful name for her. Even at this tender age, she seems to have been enticing all those who come to see her."

Prasuti laughed .When her husband began looking at her, she explained, "Her very presence is making this place unique."

"Prasuti!"

"Yes!"

"Time will decide the journey of our daughter's life."

"Even I want to tell you something."

"Speak out your mind, Prasuti."

"There is a strange depth in her eyes! She has the looks of a star!"

"Prasuti!"

"Yes, my dear husband?"

"I'll be very proud when others will call her Dakshayani..."

With a smile then said Prasuti, "Prajapati Daksha, don't be so possessive." She mused over something and then said, "One thing is very certain that she'll make this place brighter in every way...But, I fear the air of mystery about her, I don't know why!"

On that Prajapati Daksha said, "Dear wife, dispel all your doubts now and never ever for a moment forget that your husband owns the world!"

CONTENT

"Sati, what thoughts are you lost in?" Shiva asked, looking at me. Startled, I gazed at him, I feel, the great Prajapati Daksha's dear daughter isn't finding this vast solitude of Kailash very appealing!"

I could detect the humor in his tone.

"How could you sense that I'm not happy here?" I asked feigning anger.

"I haven't just said it for the sake of it, Sati."

"Why?" I asked in a slightly louder voice.

"I feel that the dull and drab life of this place isn't ideal for you."

I knew that it was his histrionics only. Even then, I asked, "Don't you know my mind... my feelings?" A silence ensued. He looked on. I began again, "Still I'm not very clear about your real meaning. I wonder what gives you this impression. Explain it to me.

Shiva laughed loudly. Seeing me confused, he said, "There are moments when I feel that a life deprived of comforts is painful. He stopped for a few moments.

His face seemed to have a tender expression then. I began musing over my own thoughts... emotions. But, startled, I came back to my own self when his loving voice floated into my ears. “Sati, the real thing is that we can’t overlook the truth. Any denial of it is the cause of suffering,” he added.

“I’m unable to understand this, my dear,” I said. He looked at me. “I want an explanation from you,” I said in a pleading tone.

“How do you find this Kailash region, Sati?” he asked, observing me.

“Your presence would make every place beautiful, my dear,” I said with utmost sincerity.

On hearing that, the lord of the universe said, “Don’t never ever forget it Sati that it’s all a desolate place here.” He stopped for a few moments. I did not speak out anything. He went on, “And don’t ever forget it either who are around you here...? Your company here...!”

“Please elaborate upon it, “I said in a serious tone.

“Don’t you ever get perturbed by ghosts and fiends, my pals and associates here?”

“No.”

“Why?”

“How can I answer it?”

“I’m much surprised at this, Sati.”

“I don’t get it!”

"All other creatures of the world are afraid of my associates and of my wild and fierce looks." I just laughed at his observation. He fixed his gaze on me and, then asked, "And now you tell me what have you been laughing at?"

"What's the use of it?" I humored."

"Why? Don't I have any right here?"

Then, watching his countenance, I said, "Now you just tell what's not known to you in this universe?"

His eyes expressed his profound love for me. Then, he said, "Sati, a doubt keeps coming into my mind often!"

"What is that?" fixing my gaze on him, I asked.

He began brooding over something. I was overcome by doubts. After a long silence, he said, "Right now I have been thinking about Daksharaj, your father!"

"What has been reminding you of him at this moment?" I asked Shiva. He cast a loving glance at me and said sotto voce, "Every parent has some aspirations for his offspring. He does his best for them. The truth is, your father, Prajapati Daksha is the king of the whole world." He paused for few moments. Even I did not utter any word then. At the end, breaking a long silence, Shiva said, "Among all your sisters you were the most loved one. However, you couldn't abide by his order. I feel, he must be very hurt within. He paused again for a few moments. Confused a lot, I did not know what to say then. He began again, "How tender and beautiful you were! You were brought up amidst all those comforts and luxuries! Where would you get those big and grand mansions and those precious things? Those sumptuous delicacies, those expensive designer dresses and that suite of servants and attendants! Here, you won't have those expansive, beautiful gardens and those wonderful things to entertain you."

He fell silent. I could finally feel his emotions. At the heart of my hearts, I was fully aware that he was very happy with my presence.

"Should I also say something now?" I said, breaking that long silence.

Casting a glance at me, he said, Sati, now you own me and all that is mine. Here you can tell me anything that you want to. Not only this much. All those who serve here are yours too. You hold the full right of giving any order to anyone."

His words had pleased me immensely. In the sweetness of those moments, I had forgotten completely that my own life had changed altogether. At my father's place, I was free..... I did not have any personal responsibility. But, now at my husband's place, I had been carrying out my uxorial duties every day.

What else was there in my life to get now after getting a spouse who was above all human weaknesses, who was beyond the hold of time and who was the lord of the whole world. Whatever I had at my father's place was shared by others too, but, here everything belonged to me. ... Also my eternal love was with me now. I knew well that my spouse was omnipotent and was capable of governing the entire Universe.

I knew well then that my sisters, their husbands, my friends, relatives and my parents could never understand that getting Shiva was my goal in life. It was my ultimate choice. He was my destiny! My life began with Shiva and was to get absorbed into it.

I was overwhelmed. His very company was the most desirable thing. Who says that Shiva is above all feelings and passions? I, Sati, too am above all emotions and passions. We are one... Totally absorbed into each other.... We are one entity only. In this Grand Union, meeting and separation are just a *leela*, an act.

The lifestyle of Kailash had irrigated my entire being.... It had seeped through my entire being. What seemed deprivation to others, was for me sweet and meaningful. Only here had I come by a completely free uninhibited and natural life. It was perfect too. It had brought to me that nearness that expands the horizon of one's life. The pleasure and tranquility that I got in these caves of ice was not available anywhere else... in those big, grand mansions and many rich lifestyles. Living at that place had cleared up my doubts. I had known by now why my spouse who was the giver of all those luxuries and prosperity and why he kept himself away from all those things.

Even great saints, sages, hermits and recluses, yogis and savants and deities, felt themselves obliged after having a glimpse of my dear Lord and, when they addressed me as 'mother', I was thrilled to the core.

Shiva would narrate to me diverse anecdotes and stories and let on all those secrets of the macrocosm.

"Sati, I want to ask you something today", Shiva said to me one day.

I said, "You can ask me anything any time. You don't have to take my permission at all."

His face was calm and serious in those moments. "Should I put up the question?" he asked.

"Here I have been waiting for you to ask the question," I said, curious.

"Will you give me an honest answer?"

"Why do you have this doubt?"

"It just came into my mind."

"What do you take me for?" I said in a slightly angry tone.

"And what do you think about me?" he himself put up a question to me.

"Don't try to fool me with your eloquence and jugglery of words," I said in a calm voice. He looked at me. My face somber, I said, looking at him sharply,

"I asked you the question first. And, now you must answer it first." He laughed. "What have you been laughing at now? Have I said something unwanted and objectionable?"

I had secretly been enjoying my dear husband's talks. And I was very sure that he too was.

"Sati!"

"What is there now?"

"You don't want to know about what I was thinking of asking you a few moments ago!"

"Now don't try to draw me into this vortex of your these glib talks," I said a little flirtatiously.

"Who can go against his wife, Sati?

"Okay, let it on", I said.

"Your excellence is even beyond my imagination," said Shiva with all seriousness. Excited and overjoyed, I just kept looked on at. "Your coming over to this place hasn't at all affected me adversely." He now stopped to muse over something. And, after a long pause, he began again, "Sati, after your coming into my life, my ascetic lifestyle has taken on a larger dimension. It appeals to others with greater intensity now." Shiva touched my forehead lovingly and tenderly.

I burst into a loud laughter. And when Shiva looked at me with surprise, I said feigning complaint, "And how you kept me waiting for reaching to this place!"

I paused for a few moments. He just kept quiet. I began again, "You had some other view earlier about this relationship! How come you have changed so much now?"

He did not speak anything for some time. His tone was extremely grave when he said, "Don't you know that everything is governed by Destiny here!"

"Are you governed by Destiny?" I asked rather bluntly.

"To abide by the rules and laws of the universe is necessary.... obligatory for all, Sati," said Shiva and, then paused for a few moments. Then, he went on again, "This is right that I'm the creator of all rules and laws; but, the truth is that even I'm bound by them and can't overlook them. Even, I have to follow them, abide by the formalities. I've got to accept their superiority.... their sanctity. They are sacrosanct at all level of existence. You must be convinced with my explanation."

On that I said "My dear Shiva, I can't ever dream of doubting the veracity of your statement and, yet, I've some reservations about them."

"Ask me anything, Sati, I'm sure whatever I tell you now, will clear up all your doubts," said Shiva.

"I love you a lot and, am immensely proud of you too," I said with a sudden surge of emotions,

"Sati, let on your thoughts. It'll give me pleasure," said Shiva, his face glowing with pleasure.

I was happy with his transparent character. I asked, "Shiva, you say you love me so much! Then, why didn't you accept all my overtures of love for a long time?" I stopped for a few moments. Shiva just kept observing my face. Maybe, he was trying to guess all that was going on in my mind. "Perhaps, ascetic and abstemious Shiva who is a yogi perfect is above all emotions and passions!"

He laughed. Then, he said, "But, now, everything is all right after all. It's the duty of all to forget the past and to devote themselves entirely into making their present. Sati, it's my request.... plea to you that you don't fritter away your time and energy by brooding over your past memories." He stopped for a few moments and began musing over something. Even I did not utter anything. I just kept looking at him without even blinking my eyes. At the end, breaking that long silence, he said, "Sati, time is the very foundation of our life.... Our future rests on our present." He paused again and his voice became very tender and passionate when he said "Your very arrival here, has transformed the ambience of Kailash. Now, I feel a new system.... a new way of life has come into existence here.... at Kailash. Whatever that was inactive and inert here till now, has become alive, activated and enlivened. There isn't anything moribund here anymore. Till now the Shiva that was lifeless and powerless has been transformed into a power-house." Once more he paused. I cast a loving glance at him. In those divine moments whatever was being transmitted and exchanged between him and me seemed to have been thrilling and delighting the entire universe. At last, Shiva spoke out, “Only your coming to this place is responsible for all these things ... events. Sati you were my eternal companion and, you’re still the one. Only you’re my true love. Only by your presence, the entire Kailash and all its inmates and objects are now imbued with its radiance.”

His words had overpowered me with great love. Entranced and overcome by emotions, I told Shiva, “My dear husband, can Shakti be separated from her Shiva?” This Sati is born only for you. You own her very life. Whoever insults you, looks down upon you, can never be accepted by Sati.... can’t belong to her in any way.....” I stopped for a few seconds. Shiva was looking at me in the very same manner. In those moments, I felt a great sweetness coursing through my veins. It was invisible and ineffable. I told him, “Your love has given me expansion. The liberation that I have been experiencing in these moments is only possible in the company of Shiva.... Only in yours,” I said to him, tenderly and in a whisper.

Although the lifestyle at Kailash was different, it was not dull and drab in any way. In the beginning I was slightly uncomfortable.... restless; but, soon it began seeming to me very colorful. Perhaps, it was so because of Shiva’s presence, Basically, the region of Kailash conveys a sense of intimacy. Its splendor was by far beautiful than the splendor of the cities built up by the humans. Here every object, every inhabitant had a natural meaningfulness-significance.

I was a mother for all there. Nandi always importuned me like a small child. Shiva's other associates pestered me too. There were moments when I would scold Nandi. They would all come to me any time and would ask for food.

"Mother I'm starving! Give me something to eat, "Nandi pleaded to me one day.

"Right now, I don't have anything Nandi," I said, faking anger. Then, I said, staring at him, "You're incorrigible. You don't seem to have any consideration towards me. And, I'd like to tell you one thing more here!" He looked at me. "Never ever forget that this is a household. Here, you've to follow certain rules. You can't have here everything's at your will. All of you make such noise at this place! I think that all of you don't know what it means to be disciplined. I wonder if I could at all take the responsibility of this rowdy family.

When I stopped, Shiva cast a sharp glance at me. A smile had come over his face. I tried to conceal my own one. "Don't scold the poor soul so much, Sati! Be kind towards him. He is not to blame for anything. His appetite is enormous and, he can't control it. Overcome by the pangs of hunger, he's always looking for some food or any other eatables."

"Now, I don't want your recommendation on his behalf. I'm convinced that, Nandi is a smooth operator," I told Shiva.

Nandi kept looking at me, his innocence was speaking through eyes. "Where should I go now, mother? he asked me.

"How can I answer that question?"

"Mother!"

"Yes!"

"I'm confused," said Nandi.

"Don't be confused. I know well now your tactics."

"Do you really want me to go away?"

Yes."

"Without any food?"

"Yes, without any food." There was an intense expression in his eyes in those moments. I went on, deliberately maintaining the harshness in my tone, "Nandi, today everything is finished. There isn't any food in my kitchen just now."

Nandi was a master in histrionics. Voice low, he said, "Okay mother! I get it now. It you don't have anything in your kitchen for your son, then, where else do I get something to eat?

At that, Shiva spoke out. "Sati, will you let your son go hungry from here? Won't it make you unhappy?"

Nandi had begun walking towards the exit slowly.

"Nandi!" I called out.

"Yes, mother" he said, turning towards me, his face looking happy.

"Now stop your dramatics!" I said, looking at him, He tried to guess my thoughts like an expert adventurer. "Sit here calmly! I'll now get you something to eat." He looked gratefully at me. I held myself back from smiling. "Now, in future don't keep gatecrashing at odd hours!"

I went to arrange food for Nandi. When, I came out the kitchen, I had the shock of my life. There, with Nandi ten more gans... associates of Shiva' were sitting beside Nandi. All of them flashed a shy smile at me.

"What's all this?" I could not even have control over my facial expressions. "Now why are you all here?"

"I must ask them, Sati! Don't get upset. I'll ask them what they want here!" said Shiva to guess my thoughts.

Before, he could ask them anything, I spoke out, "I feel, it has all been planned by Nandi!" Then, looking at them, I asked, "Why have you all come here at this time?"

"Why has Nandi come here, mother?" asked a very tall and dark-complexioned Shiva associate.

"He's hungry! I have to give him some food!" I said in an even voice.

"Mother!" a very ugly and fat associate of Shiva called out in his strident voice.

"Yes!" I said to him.

"Mother, we're all starving too!" all of them said in unison.

"Aren't you all ashamed of yourselves?"

They burst into laughter. One of them said, "Why should one feel ashamed before one's mother?"

I looked at him. His eyes had a pleading expression. All of them had that innocent, pleading look in their eyes. I could not resist that anymore. Those eyes were pure and expectant.

"Give us some food mother," once more all of them said in one voice.

My heart went out to them. In those moments, they seemed exceedingly vulnerable to me. At last, looking at them with love, I said, "Okay sons, you win and I lose! That's fine! Now quietly you wait here for some time and, I all bring some food for you. Don't indulge in rowdiness. I can't put up with your rough ways. And, in case, if you at all violate the peace of this place you won't get any food. And, you'll be punished too." I waited for a few moments. When, they began looking at me, I said, "You won't have to wait for a long time....."

...Shiva's family was now my family. I was much touched when I saw a smile on my lord's face and on the faces of all others. I saw a deep love in the eyes of Shiva then. His happiness had made me happy too. Perhaps, he was happy about my love and respect for his associates. The expression of his eyes in those moments was ineffable. Their outspokenness was not easy to guess. In those moments, I was not just his wife. I was his eternal friend, his lover from the beginning of the creation. The truth is, I was Shiva and Shiva was me. His eyes shone in the silence of the place. His associates left the place long back after having their food. His large, eloquent eyes seemed to have been expressing everything. There was a look of mute surrender in his body language. It was a great moment. The whole Creation seems to have been throbbing with a primordial rhythm. The love that had been lying buried under his indifferent exterior was now glazing brightly with that latent fire of love. It was an expansive relationship, a reaching out to the longing selves. In those moments, a male and a female had attained oneness. Even the difference between the two individuals had ended. It was just one vast consciousness in essence. Lost in my own self, in those moments I had been quietly observing the expansion of my own soul. It seemed to me then that only, Shiva and I were there. None else was around us. How intoxicating were those moments!

"What's going on in your mind, Sati?" Shiva spoke out in a very sweet and soft tone, just to bring me back to my own self.

"Nothing! Just my mind had strayed for a few moments," I said still lost in that sweetness.

"I want to give you some advice!"

"To me? Yes!"

"Try to keep a control over your mind.... thoughts," he said with a smile and in a lighter vein.

"How can I stop my mind from wandering?" He began looking at me as if was not catching on what I had been telling him in those moments. Then, in a flash, I could know what had been going on there. "Only, you're responsible for this," I said in a censorious tone.

"How do you say that?" Shiva asked."

"Don't you know it?"

"No! I don't. You tell me!" he said, requesting.

"Is it not some sort of word play on your part- A kind of bantering", I said emphatically.

"To this my answer is a big no... That's all I want to say," he said.

"It seems to be a different thing to me."

"How?"

"You have been teasing me deliberately," I said.

"This is not true, Sati. Trust me."

"I have only been trusting you."

Shiva became serious. His face shone like the sun in those moments. Then, looking at me, he said,

"Don't forget your real identity, Sati. In times to come....ages.... the saga of Shiva and SatI, love will show the path to the whole mankind. It'll be a source of inspiration to all lovers and devotees."

Those words of the omnipotent Shiva had cleared up all my doubts. All gaps between us had been wiped out. A big void had spread over the place. It was spreading over the whole Creation. And that enormous and unfathomable void was emerging from Shiva. I could make out that the infinite void was my God. I just watched on. Entranced. All of a sudden I saw.... felt that I too was there with Shiva. He spread out his huge arms before me. Walking quickly I got into them. The whole Creation was at that time echoing with the mantra of 'Om Namah Shivaya' in the air'.

Shiva was a true ascetic. He was the purest entity. He was free from any kind of deception. His character was transparent and, his activities, above board. He was my Lord, my friend and my mentor, and, above all these, he was my guide. For me, nothing existed beyond him. His company was for me better than any ygyas. It gave the benefits of multiple ygyas. The ambience that was at Kailash was pure and spiritually enlightening. When compared with the atmosphere at my father's place, it lacked in that vibrancy.

But, there were moments when in the solitude of that mountainous region, I'd begin brooding over my own past life. In the midst of all affluence, I suffered silently. There were occasions when I would be depressed for hours, for days. From my exterior, none could guess how my internal suffering had been tormenting me. The truth is that, while everyone was very happy around me, I felt annoyed by all that. In my father's magnificent and huge mansion, I felt the lack of freedom. Everything, even the inmates there, lacked the warmth of life. There were moments when I would feel if they were all just or mechanical toys; those who danced and sang at the suggestions of one hand. Sometimes, I even suffered from a guilt complex. It is because all my sisters, my parents all others would try to make me happy and fritter away their energy for nothing. All the time, they tried to fulfill all my demands. My word would be an order for them. In the moments of solitude, I would just think about my Lord Shiva. All that glory and glitter around me did not seem to have any meaning. That situation was hard to put up with. It had wounded my soul. I had been aiming to get a higher life. I knew well that it was only possible in the company of Shiva. The truth is that I was internally cut off from the life around me. My father, great Prajapati Daksha, was totally against Shiva. He abhorred his very name and condemned the people who showed any reverence for Shiva.

I was very sure that my father would never accept my love for Shiva. I also knew that he never listened to anyone's advice and always acted upon his own instincts and whims. He had very fixed and strong views against the people and situations. In his view, Shiva was no better than a cut up. However at the heart of hearts, I knew that Shiva loved me too, though, he acted as he did not want to have anything to do with me, but all females can instinctively smell the real love. So, I felt that about Shiva. I knew that his that apathy towards me was just a deliberate ruse; and when the right time would arrive, he would take me away with him to his place. The way he had been acting before others was, perhaps, a part of his leela. I also knew that time passed at my father's place was an essential part of my being and, in no case; it could be put aside and discarded. The truth is that I myself wanted to keep those cherished memories into my own being. My parents and my sisters had never been miserly in showering their love over me.

I do recall them... those memories. They were full of sentiments... feelings and very sweet gestures. Those utterances float into my ears and carry me away into the unknown lands of reminiscences. They were opulent. In that insistence, there would be a tone of authority, an authority that was born out of nearness. There were moments when those voices indicated concern... Sometimes they suggested identification and sometimes a subtle fracture between two diametrically opposite views. There was a streak of tragedy in it right from its inception. It was an unimaginable situation. All through my thought process, it existed on my mind in an embryonic form. But, it was a powerful presence. It had churned my entire being. Living with this polarity in my conscious life was a very painful thing.

❑

"Sati, how long will you be sleeping like this? Get up fast! We've to go to collect flowers! Give up this sloth-like laziness."

"Let me sleep for some more time, didi.... Don't be after my life! We'll go to collect flowers afterwards. Flowers aren't fleeing away from our us," I said, faking some annoyance.

"Do you get up or not or else, I should use my authority. I hate any sort of coercion," she said with fake harshness.

Quickly, I got up. "You're cruel and don't have any feelings," I said in a complaining voice.

"What did you say? I'm cruel!"

"She feigns being hurt."

"You woke me up in such a moment...!"

"How does it make me cruel? she asked.

I looked up at her intensely and then said, "I was seeing a beautiful dream...

A really sweet one. But you...."

I had left my sentence in the middle. Her tone had become grave. " Sati!"

"Yes, didi?"

"Do you love me? Have some respect for me?"

I was pained by her words. It was reflected in my tone. I said to her, "I'm pained. Your words have put me out!" I stopped to organize my thoughts in a more impressive way. She looked at me. Suspiciously, I began again, "How could you have that kind of doubt? Don't you know how much I love you? I look up to you. But, today in asking all that you've shattered my faith..... my confidence."

"Sati, don't feel that so much. I don't doubt you at all.... You're my dear, little sister," she said to console me.

Tears welled up in my eyes. "Then, why did you raise that doubt?" I asked my voice low and tearful.

"I'm sorry, Sati," She said again.

I said, my voice sad," I'm very hurt and cross with you."

"Don't be cross with me.... I can't put up with your moods."

I looked up at her. I fixed my gaze on her face. She looked confused. "Okay-now forget all that.... Let's be friends again. But never ever question my love for you," I said in one breath.

She did not speak out immediately. Then, she said, "Sati, no umbrage now! Perhaps, I'm a little more concerned about you. I forget that you're a grown up woman now." She stopped for a few moments. Then, she showed as if she remembered something. Looking sharply at me, she said, "Sati, now tell me what dream did you have? You were about to tell me that." She stopped to study my face. I maintained my aplomb. She told me, "Don't conceal anything from me."

"Why would I conceal anything from you?"

"I feel sometimes you do!"

"Do you?"

"Yes, I do."

"Then, I also want to tell you something!"

"Yes."

"You aren't very good at reading the thoughts of the people," I said.

She laughed. "But I can read your thoughts," she said, her voice teasing.

I remained serious. "Intentions are misconstrued by those who're near and dear to you," I said.

Then, she said in a peremptory tone, "Now tell me the whole thing!"

"I find it difficult to tell it to you,"

"Why?"

"You might take it otherwise!"

"No- I won't. Promise!" She said to assure me.

"You know that," I said laconically and with some amount of uncertainty.

On hearing my words, her face became hard and, she said in a sharp tone, "Oh! I get it now...! The very same dream!"

"Don't take it otherwise. You've promised that, haven't you? You can't back out now!" I said hurriedly.

"You must have seen the very same thing, haven't you?" she said.

I smiled. "What?" I asked, my tone humorous.

Her tone was bitter when she said, "It must have been your trisul and damru and what not..... I'm sure you must have seen all these."

Fixing my gaze on her confidently, I said, "You're right."

"But, are you aware of the consequences?" she asked.

"It isn't under my control.... I can't hold all this in," I said slowly but with a lot of confidence.

"Why isn't this under your control? she demanded.

"Who has control over love!?" I stopped and looked at her. She seemed to be at sixes and sevens. "Love is the greatest compulsion.... the worst ever dictator on the whole universe....." I waited for a few seconds. A silence had come between us. My lips spread over into a smile. "My dear, I'm love's greatest slave. Its incursions are what I can't resist... No one can. I've given myself away to it and, am very happy too," I said at one breath.

Didi kept listening to me. Shocked, she did not know much about handling that situation. But, after a long silence, she could utter, "Don't you have any consideration for personal relationships?" I did not answer the question immediately. She began again, "Should one allow love to be a destroyer?"

Her questions had made me silent. I was in a very difficult and uncertain mental state. I thought it to be the best thing to remain silent. I was quite capable of giving her an answer. But, I decided against it. I knew she loved me a lot. In no case could I even dream of hurting her emotionally. Her dignity was the most important thing for me.

At last, wanting to change the topics I said, "Okay-now tell me what to do?"

A smile came over her bright face and she said, "Now get ready as fast as you can. After that all of us can go to the garden, adjacent to the river. The clarion air there refreshes you; and, then, you're just in the midst of awesome beauty. There you're transported to the most unexpected and surprising delights of the natural world. The birds twitter all around you and keep you surprising with their colorful feathers all the time"

With a smile, I said, "You've given such beautiful details of the place that now I want to explore it with my own vision.

We had reached there. The place was filled with the redolence of the flowers all around. The sweet songs of birds had been filling the whole place with the musical notes. Those flowers with their different kinds of hues and aroma were the beautiful sight to look at.

"Let's pick up the flowers, Sati," one of my sisters said to me.

All of us began picking up those flowers.

The freshness of the air in the garden was very inspiring. The crystalline river was flowing with a murmuring sound. The verdure of the place was much as to capture our entire being. Our beautiful garments were adding to our beauty a lot. While picking up those flowers, we had been occasionally singing songs and talking and laughing too. In those moments, we were all experiencing a great joy within us.

It was a very pleasant situation. I felt very delighted. In those moments, I was overcome by a very powerful joie de vivre. Strong emotions welled up in me. From time to time, we had been giggling. All of us were infected with that jovial spirit. In those sweet moments, I was freed from any feeling of depression. At that time, I felt that relationships in the world mattered a lot. Those who are near to our heart act like a powerful catalyst. Their very contact can bring about a huge change in our psyche. Not only that much, these can also bring about a momentary forgetfulness of the other issues of your life too. It is like an opium dream, shakes you, pulls you into its invisible void, whirls you, enlarges your delitescent self in a way that creates hallucinations around you. You go down into the depths of some invisible world... to region and then pop up again just to find you loitering about some terra incognita. In your dazed state of mind, you are thrilled by seeing a beautiful, indescribable rainbow beyond the river. I was like a lost child then.

"Sati!" Rohini didi called out.

Startled, I came back to the present. All my sisters had been looking at me. They were smiling at my happy mood.

"This place is very beautiful: you forget everything else here! Even your own self," I said to explain.

At that, all of them guffawed. You've given a five explanation about that, Sati," said Rohini didi to tease me.

"I can't resist the beauty of nature!" I said rather illogically.

All of them could know that I was terribly embarrassed in those moments. They were certainly enjoying my embarrassment.

"Okay! Now forget everything! We simply love to tease you. Just that much. Nothing else," said Swati didi.

"No! don't stop it! I love all of you teasing me," I blurted out briskly.

All of them liked that.

Then, Swati didi said, "Now Sati, get back to your work. Most of the times, you avoid doing hard work." She paused. I looked at her, my eyes complaining. She began again, "Don't fritter away your time now. Pick up as many flowers as you can."

"All right!" I said and moved a little away from that group.

I had begun collecting flowers. The soft touch of those colorful blossoms felt very good. Delighted me. It honed my sensuousness. I tried to catch my own reflection in that crystalline river. The water was transparent. At that very moment, I saw something lying there. I picked it up.

It seemed to be a strange sort of object under surface. Eagerly, I picked it up. That round object was brownish in color. There were lines on it and, and all over it were punctuated round points of the size of a pin-heads. I looked at it intensely and I could not make out anything of it. It had confused me a lot. I kept it rolling it on my palm. I did not know why it had been creating waves of intense but very pleasing sensation all over my body.

Meanwhile Rohini didi had reached there. Seeing that object on my hand from a distance, she asked, "Sati, what's that in your hand?"

She had not identified the object till then.

"Look at this, didi! How charming is this beautiful

brown pearl! I haven't ever seen anything so attractive before!" I said enthusiastically.

"Let me have a look at it myself. It must be very lovely! You're so excited about it!"

Opening out my palm, I said, "Isn't it exquisite?"

She was stunned. Dumbfounded for a few moments, she could not utter a single word. I wondered why she looked so distressed after seeing that brown pearl. A silence had come over between us.

"Sati, throw it away," she said in a commanding voice. Her tone had a distressed urgency.

Very shocked, I could only utter, "Why?"

You aren't answered all the time. I don't offer any explanation. Just throw it away into the stream... river! That's all!"

There was urgency in her voice.

"Why didi? It's so attractive! If I throw it away at your advice.... command, then my heart would bleed with grief. I'll be shattered to smithereens.

"Sati, you're very stubborn! And you're stupid too!" she said, her voice resentful.

"Don't be heartless, didi!" I said my voice slightly higher.

"But, you have got to rid of it!" she insisted.

"Why?"

"Don't ask me," said Rohini didi.

"Even, I want to tell you something."

"What do you want to tell me? Shoot out!"

"I want to keep it.... The very idea of throwing it away sounds like a kind of vandalism," I said my tone openly rebellious.

"You have been insulting me," said Rohini didi, with a tinge of pain in her voice.

"I can't even dream of it, "I said, hurt by her allegation.

"Then why don't you do what I have asked you to do?"

This time her tone was acrimonious.

"Why have you been insisting on my throwing it down into the river?" I asked rather indignantly.

She did not speak out anything instantly. After brooding over something, after a considerable gap, she said, slowly but cautiously, "It's all because of your grooming."

My tone was rather harsh when I said, "What's wrong about my grooming? We have the same roots! I just wonder at your remark!"

"Yes- you're right! We've the same roots. But, grooming is altogether a different issue," she said with not a little annoyance.

"How? Tell me."

Fixing her relentless gaze upon me, Rohini didi said, watching my expressions closely, "Father loved us a lot. It can't be doubted at all. But, it was like any other father. But, in contrast to this, Sati, you were cosseted by Prajapti Daksha and his sentimental spouse". She paused for a few seconds. Then she asked, in a low but sharp, mordant tone, "Do you know what you have been holding in your hand?"

"That's a fine explanation. But, I want to tell you something here too, my beloved didi." I deliberately broke off into a pause. They had all begun looking at me. I went on, "Whatever it is, and it's just fine for me. When I've accepted it, then, discarding it would be complete immorality."

All my sisters ganged against me. They began to scold me. They were trying to thrust their combined authority over me. But, when I just stuck on to my guns, they changed their tactics. They fell into coaxing me to change my mind.

"Sati, now give up this obstinacy and do whatever is being asked of you," said Rohini didi in a very loud and peremptory voice.

"Our little sister is very cute as well as very reasonable", said Tara didi in her sweetest voice.

"Our dear sister will listen to us. I'm sure about this. No, throw it down into that stream," ordered Bharuni did.

I remained pokerfaced. Did not show any reaction. But, I was much annoyed by their meaningless insistence.

At that instant, Shurubhi didi said very sweetly to me, “Sati, now listen to me carefully.” I kept looking at her imploringly. Seeing my that expression in the eyes, she said, “Do you love your father Prajapati Daksha?”

“How dare you doubt that, didi?” I said sounding very hurt.

Before she could say anything, Aditi didi cut in, “I’m afraid that great Prajapati Daksha’s dignity will be tarnished by his own daughter. I’m much worried about all this!”

“How is it going to damage the reputation of Prajapati Daksha, didi?” I asked Aditi didi.

On that Ida did spoke out, “Don’t you know how much our father is against Shiva?”

“I know that well,” I said. “But what is the fault of this thing? It’s not to blame at all for that!”

Then, Rohini didi spoke out, “What have you been holding in your hand? Do you know what it is?” She paused and, then did not speak out a single word for a long time. Breaking a long and painful silence, she said, “This is a rudraksha. It’s related directly to Shiva. It was born out of his tear drops. I know only that much. Father will be very hurt when he sees it in your hand.” She paused again. All of us kept looking at her silently. The atmosphere had become tense. At last, she said to me, in a pleading tone, "Now give it up. Throw it away, my dear sister. We cannot hurt our own father."

"His will is supreme for us," said Bharuni didi.

I kept quiet for some time. All my sisters had been looking at me intensely. Their eyes had a pleading look. It had softened me within a lot. They were all senior to me. The thought flashed cross my mind that I could not disappoint them in any way. I had thought over all that and decided that I too was Rudrapriya I know that me- Sati was Rudrapriya. Silently I whispered to my own self,' I'm Rudrapriya'.... At that time, I decided that I should discard that rudraksha.

Looking at all my sisters, I said, with pauses, "Okay-if all of you feel so about it then, I throw it away.... What use is it of for me...!"

The faces of all my sisters brightened up. But I – Sati- Rudrapriya was bitterly crying inwardly.

Silently, I kept muttering, "O Shiva, my dear Lord ... My Rudra, you forgive your Rudrapriya. She is bound with loyalty towards her father. Once more I apologize to you.

All of a sudden, I felt a deep peace settling down within me. I could then make out that Rudrapriya's Lord had received and accepted her plea...her prayer.

❑

I had thrown.... floated that rudraksha into the flowing river. Now nothing was possible. In the beginning, I had experienced a deep peace within me. But, it lasted only for a few moments. When I was all alone in my room, I was invaded by a dark mood. I was overcome by a profound sadness. Maybe that was some kind of guilt complex my Self seemed to have been whispering to me 'Sati, what have you done....!'

'Tell me what have I done? I only asked my own Self?'

Just 'You returned the gift of Shiva because others asked you to do that!'

'Why do you think like that?' I asked my inner self.'

'Have I been thinking in the wrong way?'

'Yes-you, have been thinking in the wrong way,' I said.

'What is the truth then if I may ask you?'

'This is right that my sisters had asked me to throw away that rudraksha into the river.'

'Then.'

'But, the ultimate decision was mine!

'Don't be under any illusion, Sati!'

'I'm not confused.'

'Yes- you are!'

'No - I'm not!'

My Self spoke out, 'Okay! That's fine for me! I accept your statement.' A silence ensued. It lasted for some time. 'But, why are you looking so distressed and pained now, Sati?'

'I don't want to get involved in any controversy... I want to remain free from all complexities!

"This isn't possible, "my Self said.

'Why?'

'Only you have got to find out the answer to this why?'

'I don't like this roundabout way of speaking,' I said with a trace of indignation.

'You can't get over this suffering?'

'What proof do you have for this?'

'I know your Self.'

'I was helpless.'

'You can't understand what the suffering is!'

'I can,' he said to assure me.

'I didn't have any option!' I said

'Why didn't you have one? I'm not very, convinced with your statement... confession.'

'What doubt do you have now?' I asked in a bitter and aggressive tone.

There is something more in it.

'Something more in it?

'Yes!'

'How are going to prove it?'

'I don't have to prove anything.'

'Why not?' My tone was very bitter now.

'Let not any reservations and hindrance grow up into your mind, Sati.' There was a brief silence. 'I'm not different from you, Sati. Your remorse and pain have depressed me too.' Silence ensued.

'I know the reason!'

'What's the reason?'

'You want to be free from all social bonds. You know well how disastrous and tragic it is when love is immolated at the altar of vain, social values and ideals'.

I did not speak out anything for a few moments. I was just lost in my own musings. Then, at last, breaking a long silence, I said, "So long, a girl unmarried, can't go against the will of her parents. Do you get it?'

'I got that. Perhaps, you didn't get it.

'What didn't I catch on?' I asked the question in an indignant tone.'

'What you didn't get Sati is that you can't overlook love at any level. It might hurt you a lot if you do so!'

'But, for Love, I can't turn my back on my duties! Can't desert these at my whim... Do away with them ruthlessly. A commitment to duties is the spine of a family, a society and the world at large'.

'This is absolutely right.'

'Then, what now?'

'Compulsions pain you a lot... Restrict you in multiple ways. Depress you. Cut you up. Alienate you. Drub you. Prostrate you. Smother you. Limit you. Bind you. Gore you. Tear you apart. And, above all these, bury you under a load of doubts,' my Self said at one breath.

'I can't slight my Shiva in any way. This is unimaginable. You mustn't forget one thing.... How helpless is a woman is when she is caught between her lover and the society?'

'Sati!'

'Yes!'

'Do you know what you're in my view?'

'No! I don't know! You tell me.'

'Are you curious to know about it?'

'Yes-I'm very eager to find out!'

'I'm very delighted, Sati:'

'After seeing my painful state?'

'Not at all.'

'Then, what's all this about?"

'Try to make out?

'Don't make puzzles,' I said.

'Sati!'

'What's now?'

'You seem to be perturbed?'

'Right! You've detected it,' pausing briefly, I said. I kept quiet after that. Time passed. Then, I said, 'You were to tell me something.'

'All right! listen to me attentively. Before others, you're the daughter of Prajapati Daksha.... Sati. But, not in my view...'

'Why so?'... I asked.

'You're someone else in my opinion'.

'What am I in your view?' I asked in a grave voice now.

"Sati!"

'What's that now?'

'I want to let on something now.'

'You're after me I feel,' I said.

'Sati, don't be cross with me.'

'Why shouldn't I be?' I kept brooding for a few moments. Then, I said in louder voice, 'Today, I'll definitely find about your true identity.'

'Okay! I'm ready for it!'

'My curiosity has been impelling me to do so!'

He answered, 'Sati, I'm always with you and will be!'

'You're with me always! Expatiate upon this point. Make it clear'.

'Certainly, I'll do it.'

'Do it.'

'I'm your true Self.'

'How is that?

'Everyone has an internal world'.

'Are you my internal world?'

'This is right.'

'Then, why the hell wasn't I aware of your presence till now?'

'You have been so involved with the activities of the outside world that you could never get much, time for becoming, aware of my existence.'

'Maybe, I can do so now,' I said. 'I can appreciate your true character', I added.

'That's fine! I make it clear to you now!' The inner voice became quiet. Even I began brooding over something. The voice began again, 'There's is a battle going on between your internal world and your external world. This is also a battle between duty and love. A time will come when you'll have to make a choice between these two. A clash between love and commitment to the family is the most complex thing for human beings'.

'I want to ask you something too. Will you give me answer?'

My Self said, 'Sati, only I'm your true form... your true Self. It's not unknown to you. I know you know it.'

'Ask now what you want to.'

'I just want to ask one thing... Just one question/'

'Ask it.'

'When would I get rid of this dichotomy in me?' I asked.

'Soon.'

'What makes you so confident to say this?'

'I have not been saying anything, Sati?

'Then who has been saying it?'

It said,' Rise above your doubts first. Then focus your attention over it. Everything will be clear to you then.' A silence spread over there. Continued. I'm the innermost secret of your consciousness, Sati, my Self said.'

'What's its original form?'

'This is the suppressed voice of your rebellion.'

'I can't understand it at all.'

'You'll have to be completely conscious of... towards it, Sati. Now you try to understand... appreciate this minute... invisible element.'

I spoke out, 'How can I come out of this hurricane? 'I kept brooding over some presence near me. It was invisible though; yet, I knew that it had been silently reading my movements and my reactions. I was getting drawn towards it. I whispered to it, 'You'll have to show me my path. The one I should walk on. I'm very disturbed. Shaky. This state of uncertainty has made me unstable. There are moments when I feel that pressure on me will break me off. This everyday experience of falling apart would end my entity someday. Occasionally, I feel, that the obstinacy of my parents will be the cause of my end.' I could not speak out anything for a few moments. I was helpless then. However, collecting myself afterwards, I said, my voice low but firm and clear, 'Only darkness remains before a person who is caught up between love and loyalty.' Tears welled up in my eyes! Help me!' I said.

My immobility did not continue for a long time. Someone seemed to have been telling me, 'Sati, now the time has come when you should.... must give up your reservation. Never ever forget that real love is the best and the most opulent gift in life. Sati, don't ever forget that love alone gives motion... mobility to the entire universe. A life deprived of love is bleak and desolate and breaks one off too.'

'I feel as if a thick and inky darkness is rushing in on me from all directions. Enclosed in it, I have been tossing my limits all about vainly. It's cruel grip,' I told my Self.

You'll have to come out of it, Sati'. There isn't any option left for you now, said my Self.

'It's easier to say but difficult to do.'

'It'll become easier for you if you find out... discover your real identity and accept it completely.

'Would it be as simple?'

'No!'

'Then?'

'Who are you? Why have you come here... born in this form? Born on this inanimate, feelingless and transitory world, Sati? Whose beloved are you?

'Would you be my guru by the way?' You'll have to clear away this mist?' Should I ask you a question?'

'Ask!'

'What should I do?'

'After accepting all relationships, bonds of this world and, keeping their dignity into consideration, you cannot, even then, ignore the dignity of the eternal love, Sati... Who're you my dear one...? Adi Shakti: Sarvabhutesh, Shaktirupen, Sansitha'... Neither do you have a beginning, nor do you have an end... you are eternal... And, now your foremost duty is to go beyond relationships and be one with that entity whose very motion spins the entire Creation into functioning so perfectly! Sati, don't even forget that for a moment that you're Rudrapriya. Don't even forget this too, you Parashakti that without you, in your absence, Shiva is just a corpse... Even the sound of the feet of the Natraj Shiva, his dancing gesture, his beauty and all his attributes and proclivities are imperfect and non-functioning without you. Not only this much, even the reverberating sound, notes of his damru, and, even the destructive force of his trisul get their motion from you. You activate the inert Shiva and all other elements in this universe.'

Cutting his talks in the middle, I said, 'Now just keep quiet... Don't utter anything further. All won't make out anything of this complex and invisible mystery that pervades the Macrocosm. Who would be able to perceive this vastness with one's physical eyes? There is one more thing to tell you...'

'What's that?'

'You know it.'

'Tell me.'

'When the right, auspicious time comes then all worldly ties would be severed spontaneously... without any efforts', I said.

'Any expectation in the world means to invite pains and troubles to you. Our relationships here are limited... finite. At their, roots exist pride and selfishness.

'My father, Prajapati Daksha's love for his children cannot be looked at with doubts", I said.

My Self said, 'You have told the truth, Sati. Even then I'd like to tell you that many activities of Prajapati make them questionable. And, never ever express your affection... love for Shiva before him', either.'

'Why?' I asked with a smile.'

'You aren't aware of it?'

'No! I'm not!'

'It's hard to 'believe!'

'Trust me! Because of my love for my father, I'm unable to see his demerits!' I said.

My Self said, 'All thoughts that are formed within me, are yours only, Sati.'

'This is the truth... the real thing. I began brooding over something. After a brief pause, I said, making everything clear, 'He loves me most: and, in no case, do I want to make him suffer.' I can't cause any pain to him and be a sinner.'

Then spoke out my Self, 'Keep my words on your mind, Sati. Always remember that you'll have to change your view one day. Could make your Lord, Shiva suffer in any way? Rudrapriya, you can't! The future would seek guidance from you! Be inspired by your conduct of today! They would call this Shiva Leela. A time would come when even Prajapati Daksha would be compelled to accept Shiva's greatness!'

On that, I said, 'Right now, it doesn't seem to have any possibility. But who can predict what has been lying in the womb of future! For me these moments are very painful! At present my soul is divided by a clash between two opposite emotions. It's constantly dividing my energy...., The light within me is fading out...'

My Self then spoke out, 'Sati, now forgetting everything... putting it aside, you just begin listening to your inner voice. Let it be your guide and mentor. It'll engender a new approach towards the issue... a dynamic and unconventional thought. Also, it'll give maturity. Make you pragmatic. It'll enable you to discern the reality of the situation and state of the issues and things. But, I feel, the final victory would be of love. The power that you want to belong to, will be yours someday. In this corporeal world whatever difficulties, ordeals, you've to go through, you'll be the victor at the end. A union between Shakti and Shiva gives meaning to the world, to the Creation.'

❑

With the passing of time, my love for Shiva intensified too. Perhaps, my mother and my father did not have the least idea of the depth of my feelings. Yes, it's true that my sisters often kept warning against it. Mainly, Rohini didi was concerned about it most. She would often, whenever she got a chance, tell me how our father, Prajapati Daksha was very angry with my Rudra. There were general factors ... reasons for it. Or they could be. The outsiders kept guessing about these. They say that once Shiva was angry with my grandfather- Brahma, father of Prajapati Daksha and, then Shiva cut off his one head. They also say once when Prajapati Daksha entered his Rajdarbar, the royal court-Shiva did not rise to show respect but kept sitting. He did not get up. My father took that up for his insult at a personal level. Besides these, my father also did not approve the lifestyle of Shiva. He found it degusting and reprehensible. Moreover, my father did not like Shiva's followers... associates: those demons and other spirits. In his view, they were all rowdies and nothing more. He abhorred them.

There must have been some other reasons too. Some others say, there was once a time when Prajapati Daksha did not have any enmity against Shiva. Here I would like to state with absolute objectivity that my father had no idea about the Cosmic Form of Shiva. There could be any reason for it. But, I feel, he had become very proud of his status and glamorous royalty. Overcome by his pride, he could not evaluate the worth of the people and objects. I think it had dulled his reason to the extent that he was unable to perceive the reality and its multiple expressions.

It was a very complex and tough situation for me. Neither could I look down upon my father nor could I give up my love. I was the true lover of Shiva- my Rudra. All the time, I just kept thinking about him. I would visualize him to be my life partner. I would dream of our marriage.

... I had to face all sorts of difficulties. Even if I kept all my feelings and thoughts secret, I would feel that all around me the atmosphere was becoming hostile. There were moments when I would be lost completely in my own reverie. It was beyond my own power to work against my own self. Although I made sincere efforts at times to get over my obsession with Shiva, I could not get any success in my efforts. So, after all efforts, I gave up fighting against my own instincts. I let myself go. It brought about a sense of great relief. That was the time when I realized by suppressing and by fighting against one's true self, was the most tragic thing in the world and, could shatter one's being completely. We are what we are. In this uncertain world, getting happiness is perhaps not an easy task.

There were moments too when all alone and sitting and brooding in the solitude of my own room, I wondered whether my own rebellion at my house had any meaning in the midst of those unfeeling and unsympathetic people. I had no doubts about their love and vast feelings towards me. All of them were so attached to me. Someone had advised my mother to allow me freedom to a certain extent but not so much as to make me forgetful of all norms of ideal conduct.

I had heard my mother talking to her very close friend, Chandramala, accidently. My mother was a quiet person. She was indifferent to all that, that was not approved by her husband Prajapati Daksha.

"Chandramala, I'm very cross with you," said my mother to Chandramala.

"Why, Prasuti?"

"Haven't you been my childhood friend?"

"Yes, so what?"

"You're very insensitive," said my mother to Chandramala.

"Now don't be so bitter, Prasuti. Tell me all that you want too. I can make out from the expression of your face that something has been bothering you for a long time!"

Looking straight into Chandramala's eyes, my mother told her friend, "I have here all the wealth of the world that a woman could wish for!"

"Prasuti, you don't have to tell me all this! It's very clear to anyone." She paused for a few moments. "And, why shouldn't you have all these things here? After all you're the wife of the great Prajapati!"

"That's fine~ but, I can't share my problems with every one!" blurted out my mother.

"At least you could with your husband!"

"Can't."

"Why, Prasuti!"

"It only concerns him."

"Really! What's that?"

"He's a caring husband and a doting father," said my mother.

"I know you love your husband a lot," said Chandramala with a tinge of jealousy.

"Now don't talk to me in that special tone of yours," said my mother.

"What's my special tone, Prasuti?"

"You have been taunting me about something, I don't know clearly."

"Prasuti!"

"Yes, Chandramala!"

"Forget all these things and tell me everything clearly and in detail."

"It's about my husband and about my youngest daughter, Sati",

"I'm ready to listen to you/"

"But keep it to yourself," said my mother in a choked voice.

"You don't have to tell me that. Don't forget how we would share innumerable secrets during our childhood!"

"How sweet were those days, Chandramala!"

"Don't make me sentimental, Prasuti!"

"My husband is very proud and stubborn."

"Why shouldn't he be?"

"How do you justify that? It's not at all clear to me?" said my mother, her tone was slightly sharp.

"Don't forget that he is Prajapati Daksha!"

"It doesn't give you a license to go around insulting all and insulting them with your most demeaning words," said my mother, her tone slightly bitter.

"My dear Prasuti," said Chandramala, "status is the greatest intoxicant in the world. A big and powerful person cannot put up with a differing voice. And, this is what calls for adjustment and discretion at all levels." She paused to organize her words. My mother was looking at her friend with a look that suggested a kind of request. Looking at my mother sympathetically, Chadramala said, "For her own peace and peace at her household, a woman has got to be diplomatic. By transforming her bitterness and feeling of hurt into an outward acceptance of male authority and by an outward display of submissiveness and surrender, a woman begins playing the role of a true dictator."

"I don't catch on, Chandramala."

"You have always been dim-witted, Prasuti!"

"Nonsense!"

"Just try it, and your problem will be solved within no time."

"It can't."

"Why?"

"I haven't told you the full thing.....!"

"Okay - then tell me the full thing."

"The problem isn't just related to my husband!"

"Who else is it related to?"

"My daughter!"

"Your daughter?" Chndramala paused and smiled. "You have so many of them, Prasuti!"

"It's about my youngest daughter, Sati."

"Sati! She's so sweet-tempered!"

“But she has inherited stubbornness from her father... She’s uncompromising,” said my mother to her friend.

Now don’t be harsh upon that sweet darling. In my view, she’s the sweetest and the softest,” said Chandramala, her face Sombre now. She looked at me closely. At last, she said, “Sati, in my view, is very compassionate and full of discretion. I love her.”

“You’re right, Chandramala! She’s full of discretion! But, now, the way she has been behaving, makes her full of indiscretion,” said my mother, her voice sad.

“How do you justify that?”

“She has fallen in love!”

“Really, Prasuti! Congrats!”

Don’t congratulate me.”

“Why?”

“I’ll tell you.”

“Tell me. But, who’s the lucky person.?”

“Shiva.”

“Shiva!”

“Congrats, Prasuti!”

“I don’t want your good wishes on this issue!”

“I’m shocked and surprised at that! Can you explain that to me?”

"Great Prajapati Daksha doesn't appreciate it, Chandramala.

"This is unfortunate."

"Why do you say so, Chandramala?"

"Irreverence!"

"Now why have you been using these words? You're my friend!"

"Friendship is one thing but, my dear Prasuti, truth is above all other things."

"Chandramala, I request you to enlarge upon your casual and imperfect remark. I don't want to lose a friend."

Her voice loud and her face grave, said Chandramala, "Your daughter's marriage with Shiva would add to your status a lot. But, here you have been indulging in negative thoughts!"

"How do you vindicate this big statement of yours, Chandramala?"

Chandramala did not speak out immediately. She brooded over her words for a long time. Then, with extreme reverence, she said, "My dear Prasuti, either you don't know the truth, or you have been indulging in an act of false ignorance, when you say you don't know. It almost sounds like a deliberate falsehood."

My mother said, "Chandramala I can't put up with it any longer. You must explain it all. I demand so as your childhood friend. And, don't forget that my daughter is your daughter too."

Then, becoming very serious, said Chandramala, "Prasuti, Shiva owns the entire Creation. He's the most powerful entity is known to all. Your daughter Sati's marriage with him would be the greatest event in the entire universe. She paused and looked at my mother with a caressing glance. Then, holding her hands, she began again, "You must persuade your husband to give his consent."

"This is impossible!" said my mother.

"It means a tragic thing!"

"How?"

"You know your daughter well?"

"I think I do."

Chandramala laughed." Don't remain under any illusion!"

"We aren't under any illusion!" said my mother.

"You'll be frustrated! Don't act upon any foolish idea of yours. Nothing can stand between and against your daughter and her ultimate love, her Shiva, my dear."

"We'll change her mind!"

"You can't!"

"Why can't we?"

"Her lover owns everything."

"You talk foolishly!"

"You seemed to be a narrow minded and prejudiced devotee, Chandramala!"

“I’m disturbed!”

“Why are you disturbed?” asked my mother.

“I have a sense of foreboding that your household will fall apart! You must save it, Prasuti... Let there be a truce between the father and the daughter.”

“I can’t do so!”

“Why?”

“Both are incorrigible, Chandramala!”

“I’m pained... What’re you going to do now?”

“I don’t know.”

“I can tell you.”

“Tell me, Chandramala.”

“Support your daughter in her mission.”

“Impossible!”

“Why is it impossible, Prasuti?”

“Don’t you know the tradition of this country, Chandramala?”

“You tell me.... I have my own idea about it. But, all the time. I want to hear it from your own month.”

My mother said her voice now very clear and firm, “In this country, nothing exists beyond a commitment to your husband... A husband is everything for a wife. Only by her unshakable devotion to her husband can a wife make her life pure and meaningful. A husband is a giver of everything to his wife. He’s the supreme entity in her household.” My mother stopped for a few moments, groping for more powerful words, then, breaking that long silence, she began again, “A woman’s temple is her household. Her first and foremost duty is to keep it organized and, also, to feed all those who depend on her generosity.” My mother stopped again, her face shining and confident. In those moments I fell in love with her. She seemed to be a paragon of womanly glory. Then, looking at her friend, she went on, “Chandramala, listen to me intently. I’m a wife. I’m proud of my status. At this point, remember one thing more for your own betterment.” Chandramala looked at my mother. My mother’s face had put on a divine expression. Her eyes seemed to be like two burning lamps now. She said again, “Nurtured in the opulent traditions of this most ancient country, I say to you with the utmost honesty that here when a woman accepts her life partner’s authority meekly, it’s not her passivity, it’s her acceptance of profound and incomparable traditions.”

In those moments Chandramala seems to be awestruck. For a few moments, she did not even know how to react. She had seen my mother’s that image for the first time. But, even from my own spot, I could make out, she was very pleased with my mother’s, outburst. In those moments, I also felt as if my own heart was warming up towards her.

At last, Chndramala took my mother’s hands into hers. Her voice sweet and her eyes glowing with love, she said, "Prasuti, I'm very happy with your explanation of womanhood today. Your words have given me a new light into the true meaning of woman's inherent glory. Now, I know well any rejection of masculinity of a man, doesn't make a woman a revolutionary or a rebel. In contrast to this, acceptance of masculinity lifts her up to a higher point of existence. In the process of her surrendering herself to the appropriate power, spiritualizes her and bestows upon her the role of a creator too. The truth is that in this extremely well designed world, together, the opposite forces produce a huge orchestration. This is what we call the rhythm of the universe. This is Om—the original all containing sound in the universe." She paused and began looking at my mother. "Do you want to tell me the secret of this vastness, Prasuti?"

"Yes! Chandramala explain it to me. I trust you. I love you. You churn me to surrender." She paused and flashed a smile at her friend. "You're a convincing logician," she added.

"Whatever you've told me today has touched my heart. Now, it has been coursing continuously through my veins. I feel exalted. I want to tell you one more thing." My mother looked at Chandramala. Chandramala's face had put on a serene expression. Gazing at my mother intensely, she said, "Prasuti, this is the time to move on. Life demands the process." She stopped again, musing over something.

She broke the silence at the end and said, "You must know one thing at the end of all these talks that your daughter, Sati is born to be the spouse of Shiva. Also remember one thing here that, it's something preordained and no power in the universe can stop it from happening." She paused again when my mother began looking at her. I haven't been saying that for the sake of it.

"How can you be so certain about it?" asked my mother.

Chandramala said with a smile, "Once, the great sage Narad had been explaining to some other rishi about Sati's relationship with Shiva, I was there and I could hear all that myself. That was when I came to know about the divine plan of bringing your daughter closer to Shiva. This union is meant for the preservation of spirituality in life and the universe. Now it's our duty as well as mission to co-operate with that planning."

❑

My Rohini didi was a very sensitive person. Even trivial incidents upset her a lot. After any unpleasant event, she kept brooding over it for hours. She was very pure-hearted.

One day when I was all alone in my room, she had come to me.

"Welcome, didi," I greeted her with warmth.

"Thanks!"

"I'm very happy!" I said.

"What are you happy about?"

"Seeing you is my pleasure."

A sad smile came over her face. "But, I'm very unhappy today, Sati!"

"What are you unhappy about?" I asked, very surprised.

"About events at this place," she uttered incoherently.

"I don't make out much of your words!" I said to her.

"It's because you aren't concerned!"

"What have you been accusing me of, didi??

"I haven't been accusing you of anything." She paused. I looked at her, confused. Then, she said," I must demand something from you today, Sati!"

"Don't hesitate.... you own me."

"Thanks!"

"Don't doubt my words."

"I don't," she said, holding my hands tenderly.

"Your love overwhelms me, didi"

"You're my most lovable sister, Sati."

I tensed. Because whenever she talked in that soft tone of hers, she had some serious issue on her mind.

"Do you want to tell me something?" I asked weakly.

"Yes!"

"Be frank."

"This is the moment that you begin thinking about our dear father," she said in an even tone.

"You think, I'm indifferent to him?"

"That's for you to decide. I don't want to be judgmental. You've your own mind."

"You make it clear to me, didi."

"I'm afraid of the consequences."

"Don't be incomprehensible."

"You've created a void in this place, Sati."

"Make it clear now. I can't put up with this confusion anymore," I said, "What are you afraid of?"

"I'm afraid of the consequences of your love!"

"Why so?"

"You know it, Sati."

"I want to hear it from your mouth, didi. I demand a convincing explanation," "Okay-as you wish it."

"Don't indulge in any word-play," I said to warn her.

Her face serious, she mumbled out," I'm afraid of your love."

"How do you back up your statement?"

"You know that, Sati!"

"Even then, I want to hear it from you," I told her.

"To me, love between Shiva and you seems to be destructive."

"How?"

"That you ask your own self."

"It doesn't seem so to me," A pause followed. I kept quiet for a few seconds. Then, I said, "Everything seems to be so quiet here, didi. Very normal too."

"Does it seem normal to you? "She stopped and casting a sharp glance at me. Then, she said, "Tell now, it seems to be so. But..."

"But, what?" I asked.

"Your marriage with Shiva would be the greatest insult to our father, Sati."

"Why?"

She then said, "He hates Shiva's lifestyle."

"Every person has different views, values and life-style. And, these should be so too. If all have the same one, then, won't this monotony be boring?"

She had come all prepared that day. "Don't the parents have any right over their own children?"

"They hold absolute right over them, didi."

"Don't they love their children?" she asked, her tone slightly bitter.

"It can't be questioned at all," I said.

"Do you find Prajapati's love for us in any way flawed?"

"Not at all!"

"Then how is this possible, Sati?"

"What's that?"

"You shouldn't even dream of any alliance with Shiva!"

"Impossible!"

"Why is it so?"

"My life is meaningless without Shiva, "I said, my voice sharp and stable.

"How do you justify your claim?

"Shiva is the nucleus of my life's mission. I'm Rudrapriya... his eternal lover... Nothing else." I paused for a few moments, groping for appropriate words." To get his love, I can give up anything in the world," I added.

"Sati! What sort of obsession is this? I can't make out anything of it right now. At this moment, I'm only worried about the relationship between you and our father," she said quietly.

In those moments, it became very clear to me that she loved me immensely. Her love was very transparent.

I moved forward and, then taking her hands into mine, I said emotionally, "How much you love your sister, didi!" I paused. Then peeping into her eyes, I said, "Don't be afraid about the future, my dear one. Dispel any dejection that you have in you. Your sister isn't just an ordinary lover... She's Rudrapriya. Her foremost goal in life is to win over the love of Shiva... Rudra. I have been looking for his eternal love...." I paused. Rohini didi just looked on at me with a very strange expression in her eyes. In those moments, it became very clear to me that it was beyond her mind to appreciate the true depth of my love... The truth is that all cannot know the infinite vastness of love... Then, to console her disturbed mind, I said, "Now, be relaxed, my darling sister. In no case... situation am I going to cross the desired and prescribed limit.

My own parents are my gods. I can't make them feel small in any way."

Her face brightened up. Casting a caressing glance at me, she said, in her sweetest tone, "That's fine, Sati. I'm answered. "I trust your discretion."

"Thanks, didi!"

"Now why do you have to thank me?"

"I'm overpowered by your profound love. How much you think about me!"

"This love is spontaneous, Sati!"

"Didi!"

"Yes, Sati!"

"You are love incarnate!"

"You too are the same," she said, laughing softly.

"Ask it."

"Will you give me an honest answer?"

"I'll try that."

"I just don't want only trying!"

"Then, what do you expect from me?" Rohini didi asked.

"I want an answer from the very depths of your heart.

"Okay-ask it."

"Not just like that!"

"Then, what else do you expect now?"

“You make a promise.”

“If I make a false promise, then?”

“I know well that you can never prevaricate....”

She was overcome by love and emotions in those moments. With efforts, she could just mumble,” Do you trust me that much?” She paused. I looked at her. A smile had spread over her cherubic face.” How do you vindicate that?”

“I don’t have to justify the veracity of my personal view... You know the reason, “I said to her.

“Honestly speaking, Sati, I’m not aware of it.... Tell me... I request you!”

“Speaking the truth is a part of your character.”

“Thank you, Sati, “she said, her fare suffused with happiness.

“I’ve one more observation to make about you didi.”

“Sati!”

“Yes, didi?”

“You’re a complex person. You never let on your secret... Now shoot out what you have on your plotting mind.”

I laughed. I was very amused by her statement. “Do you want me to let on my secret thought...? It might aggravate you, and you’ll then curse me freely, “I told her in an amused manner.”

“I can’t wait any more, Sati. Tell me.”

"Your face is like a big mirror. It gives the complete view of the interior to a real observer, "I said appreciatively.

She smiled. My talks had dispelled the darkness within her. Even then, she asked, "You think that you're a very accomplished face-reader, don't you?"

"I am."

"Okay- I accept it. Then, what can I do about it?"

"Nothing!" I said rather sentimentally.

"Don't you think, it's a kind of weakness?"

"No! I don't think so!"

"Can you justify your statement?"

"I can, didi."

"Please do it for me, Sati."

"It makes you different from others, my sweet girl! You aren't even aware of your greatest strength, "I uttered with pauses and in a low voice.

"But your jijaji Chandra, feels that I shouldn't be told any private thing... He feels that I'm not quite mature to keep a secret," said Rohini didi with a tinge of sadness.

"Didi!"

"Yes, Sati?"

"I want to tell you one thing."

"Tell, Sati."

"Keep it to yourself only."

"I won't tell anyone. Trust me!"

"I don't want to share my thoughts with any one at all, didi."

"I know, Sati that you love me a lot."

"Did you have any talks with our mother and father?"

"About what?"

"About me only!"

"Why?"

"They worry a lot about me."

"This is natural, Sati."

"How do you say that?"

"You're the most loved one among all their daughters. Besides that, you're the youngest one too, but, now, you're a grown woman."

"How does it matter?"

"Now, all the time, they have been worrying about your marriage."

"I want to tell you something more, didi."

"Don't wait now... Tell it!"

"I don't want to get married," I said without raising my voice.

"Why? It's the dream of every girl... Then, why don't you dream of it? It seems abnormal to me!" said Rohini didi, looking very confused in those moments.

"You know that already, "I said, sotto voce.

"Even then you must tell me."

Then, I said, "Didi, if I at all get married, it'll be my Shiva-my Rudra only. No one else. I'll remain unmarried otherwise."

"What's that Sati? Will you go against your own father?"

"Prajapati Daksha is under the worst delusion at present, didi!"

"Such a big charge against him, Sati. How are you going to support your observation?"

"I can back it up with convincing argument, "I said in a steady voice.

"How? Then do so right now?"

"Once our grandfather, Brahmdeva, the creator of this universe said in my presence to Prajapati Daksha, "Son, try to differentiate between pride and self-respect. I fear that your overlooking it may cause you to fall into the nadir of decline and degeneration. And, remember it, when this downward slide begins, you won't even be aware of it." Our grandfather's wise words and expostulation didn't leave any impression upon our father," I said.

Quietly, Rohini didi listened to me. Her face was quite excited when she said, "How pure is the ambience of this place! Just look at this huge and magnificent idol of Lord Vishnu here! Our father had it installed with great thoughtfulness. I feel, it has enhanced immensely the glory of this place! It has given it a unique dignity." She paused and groped for more effective words. The moments passed. Then, at last, she spoke out, "The presence of these erudite, eminent saints and savants cannot be overlooked. Listen to the sweet chanting of mantras by the learned pundits and brahmins. All rituals performed here create in you an awareness of the vastness of the spiritual world. And, don't forget that unveiling of the statue of Lord Vishnu! It seems to have transformed the whole place into a temple. Also it evokes a sense of purity and security in all inmates of this place!"

"Didi!"

"Yes, Sati?"

"I congratulate you!"

"What do you congratulate me for?"

"All your utterances sound like poetry!"

"Really?"

"Your husband, Chandra, must be very proud of you!"

"Why do say so?"

"There is some reason for it, " I said.

"What's your reason?" asked Rohini didi.

I smiled, "Your utterances are enchanting," I said.

She was very amused. Then, she said, laughing, "Sati, I also want to tell you something now." I began looking at her with a questioning look. She went on, "Our father wants to have a very grand function at your marriage." She paused and then said in a low tone," Will it ever be possible, Sati?"

"Why do you doubt it, didi?" I paused for a few moments." I think our father is very fond of big, grand gatherings and parties."

"You're right, Sati. But, I'm very afraid of the intensity of his anger. The truth is that he gets the utmost satisfaction when he runs his own affairs. He doesn't want to have any view against his own. This is what I fear the most."

❑

I was reminded of the scene of the unveiling of the idol of Lord Vishnu. Proudly then said, Prajapati Daksha, my father, "Today, before this gathering, I want to say that I have been given the charge of running the system of this world. Only, I've to take care of its smooth functioning. I hereby assure you all that I'll carry out all my duties to the best of my ability. And, reclining on the bed of the Sheshnag, Lord Vishnu will keep giving us inspiration... This idol of his."

But some rishis (Saptrishis) present looked worried. They felt that the idol of Lord Vishnu there was imperfect. There was definitely some flaw in that. At least, they were not very happy about it. Even the sky had darkened then.

Prajapati Daksha had then said, his voice full of pride, "In this world only the human beings take care of others. But, I've a greater responsibility. I've to look after the very modality of the world. I've to set up the rules and regulations. Streamline the systems. "He paused and looked around. All present there, had been listening to him intently. Happily, he began again, "Today's function is related to it too. Through this idol, I've set up the modalities of the world." I was very upset. All those saints and savants present there in seemed to be in a state of uncertainty. Prajapati Daksha's voice echoed again through that place, "Today, I've reached the highest point of my responsibility. The idol of my object of devotion, Lord Vishnu, has been set-up. No longer is this now just an idol. It confirms my vision and, also it justifies my norms and life-style. Today, I announce it... declare it before you that Lord Vishnu is the supreme God among gods. Only he's the Parmeshwar of the entire universe.

Shocked, I kept listening to him. I did not make out much of his that empty speech. It was insubstantial in every way. I had closed my eyes. I was absorbed into some infinite void. I was a lost being, in those moments, I felt like that. Every object... structure of the universe seems to be vanishing into it. All animate and inanimate objects seemed to have been existing only in that eternal, limitless emptiness... naught. It contained all. The All was contained in that only. In those specific moments, I realized that it was the true divinity. That infinite void was Shiva... divinity. Only Shiva. Here only our longing and desiring instincts and physical efforts come to rest ultimately.

How did that eternal void affect me? I was totally absorbed in my beloved Shiva. I felt his presence all around me, in me too. I was thrilled. Exulted. Lost. Drowned. Churned. Stretched. Expanded. Spiritualized. Astounded. Endowed. Bestowed upon. Enriched. Categorized. Specified. Generalized. Personalized. Socialized. Pained and delighted. Dehydrated and empowered at once. In me was then born that expansion of awareness that enabled me to perceive the true glory of Shiva and of my own Self. Maybe, that point of my existence was the beginning of my process of reaching my own Shiva. It was a fresh Odyssey. That vast expansion of my true Self was just a process towards reaching my beloved Shiva. It was a state of perceptivity. A divine movement it was. I was now becoming capable of perceiving Shiva in his true essence: Shiva who does not exist and the one in whom all things exist. He is endless. He alone is the creator of this vast, limitless void. The truth is, perhaps, he himself is the creator of this void. He is not a physical entity. Nor is he any specific entity. He is The Unknowable... The Indescribable. I had found out my true entity. I was nothing else but only Shiva. I was now completely absorbed into that infinity. How beautiful, intoxicating was that union. All physicality had vanished in those moments. I had been transformed into Shivangi.

... I had become non-existent. A thick, impenetrable darkness was emanating from that void. I could now know that darkness alone was the source of all our energy. Shiva is called Rudra too. It means that who has a terrible look. Shiva in his terrible form and, I, who am born out of... exist in that energy... that is born out darkness was Shakti. Only a union of Shiva and Shakti is responsible for creating everything.

Why is Shiva also called Rudra? It is because the meaning of Shiva is that does not exist. When he is sleeping, I just keep watching him. I want to entice him. He is totally unaware of my intention. I try to persuade him. I want to dance with him. He is very annoyed when he is disturbed in his sleep. He growls. Then, angry beyond words, he quickly gets up and roars so loudly that I have given him the name Rudra. It means the one who roars very loudly. I love that name. After that whenever I sat down at my Pooja of Shiva, I called it rudrabhisek.

From this roar of Shiva, is born yoga. It begins from the region of the Himalaya. Because of this the great practitioners of and yoga luminaries went to live at the region of the Himalaya.

Then, Yoga was the essential and inseparable part of the lifestyle and everyday existence. Those wanting to comprehend the quintessence of life have got to practice yoga. It is the ultimate system in life. The first entity started the practice of yoga with the main seven sages. These enlightened souls developed evolved the system of yoga for setting us free from the entanglement of life. However, it all has its origin from Shiva only.

Shiva is also called Trinetra... Trayambaki because of his third eye. His third eye is totally different from our physical eyes. His third eye is extraordinary. It can destroy and also, it is capable of seeing... perceiving the entire Creation. Our own two physical eyes cannot look beyond a certain distance. Once these two physical eyes of ours are closed, we are overcome by blindness. We cannot see anything. We are enwrapped in darkness. The truth is we have a third eye too within us and, only in some specific moments do we become aware of its existence in us. This is a different dimension of our evolving consciousness. Once this third eye opens within us, then we can see through the whole Creation that exists within us.

The capability of seeing within one means a change in the outlook. We begin looking at the world, events, people and all objects from altogether different angle. It elevates us to a higher level. It expands our energy. A transformation of the self begins taking place within us. This third eye is the symbol of our spirituality. It sets us free from the snares of maya. Our physical eyes entangle us into the complexities of the worldly temptations, but, our third by expanding our self and, by bestirring upon energy, makes, us aware of Shiva. This is all very transparent. Whatever, we perceive through our physical eyes have severe limitations. The truth perceived through them is imperfect. Only by moving away from the gross to the subtle can we reach Shiva. Our world is a creation of three elements... attributes- tamas, rajas and sat. The world created by these three attributes is just non-existent... It's an illusion. Caught up in its temptations and allurements, we lose our capability of perceiving the true form of Shiva. We begin living the life of a parasite. The insignificance and impermanence of this corporeal world can only be known through this third eye...

I call Shiva som too. It means the moon (it is Chandra- the masculine gender in India). Shiva has placed it on his jata (matted hair). It also stands for intoxication. We cannot get it from the outside element. It is derived from the subtle spiritual process that has been going on quietly within us. The objects of the outside world cannot give us happiness.

Chandra is considered to be lacking in energy. Shiva has just put it on as a crown-the adornment piece. The greatest yogi, Shiva who is always absorbed in the intoxication of an energetic and conscious lifestyle, is above all kinds of worldly pains and tribulations.

...Shiva's vahan (carriage) is Nandi. He is a bull when he carries his Lord to some place, on his other occasions, he is in his human from. He holds a very high place in Hindu mythology. Some devotees take him for a god. Nandi is the symbol of eternal waiting. He is also a symbol of infinite patience. He is the best example of it. He does not know when the great Lord would wake up from his meditation. He does not even know when Shiva will come and go. Thus, waiting for Shiva like that makes Nandi a yogi too. He possesses the great knowledge. He is a fun-maker too. He makes the life at Kailash vibrant and entertains all its inmates with his antics. Through him you can reach Shiva. The purity of his character is unquestionable. He is also a symbol of stability and great strength. He is an indispensable part of the life at Kailash.

... Shiva adorns himself with the necklace of a poisonous snake. One day when I observed how it was making some movements slowly, at that very instant, I could know that it could not be separated from his self. It was a part of his life—being. By placing a snake on his body, Shiva has raised its status very high; otherwise, it would just wriggle on the earth. This is also true that snakes have some sort of divinity in them according to the Hindu cores tradition. In case, you don't create any threat to them, man and snake can get along well.

Om Namah Shivay is a powerful mantra to reach Shiva. It refines the body and soul and, by purifying the self of the practitioner, it brings him close to the divinity.

Travelling through the darkness of ignorance, we reach Shiva. Just beyond our own self-centeredness is the realm of radiance and beauty. Darkness is nothing but just the absence of light. The vastness of dark cannot be imagined by any one easily. Darkness is eternal. It frightens everyone. But, those who are not afraid of it and, are willing to explore it, come by wisdom at the end. It is an ocean and you need mental stability to swim through it. Just beyond it, is the realm of assurance. Those wanting to realize spirituality in its essence should plunge head long into the ocean of darkness before them. It will not be washed away. It will help a seeker to reach Shiva.

...Seven chakras in body relate to seven states of the being. These represent seven points in the body. It begins from the serpent-shaped Kundalini situated at the root of the spinal cord. As it begins moving up, it passes through some other points. The other end—the upper end is called sahasrar-chakra. If the practitioner has reached that state, he is then in control of the highest spirituality. I came to know about it only by practicing in myself. From Mooladhar to Sahasrar my journey was for establishing an endless communication and companionship with Shiva. Only at that point of realization did I have a true glimpse of my loved one. The reaching of the seventh chakra is the highest attainment.

Life is a complex unit. Spirituality cannot be defined in a material sense. Very few of us know how even Brahma, The Creator and Vishnu, the Preserver came into being. In fact Shiva is the only being who has neither a beginning nor an end and he alone is responsible for the existence of the other two Gods.

Once Shiva thought of bringing into existence someone who was expert in all branches of knowledge and who could look after the universe. He then looked at his left side and a blue complexioned entity was born. He was Vishnu.

Vishnu then sat down for a profound meditation and when he sweated, a river flowed out from there. From his navel region a lotus sprouted. It had several petals. From this very Lotus Brahma was brought into being. His complexion was red and he had faces in all four directions. He had several names but I loved the name Brahma the most.

Once Brahma wanted to find out where the roots of the lotus-flower were situated as he was curious to know about his father. So, Brahma ripped between the stem of the flower and floated through the river. For several years went on floating like that but could not reach the source of that. It went on for hundred years. Then, dejected he came back. He could not even then find out the lotus flower that he had been sitting on earlier. At that very moment Vishnu had reached there too.

"Who are you?" Brahma asked Vishnu.

Vishnu answered, "Don't you know me?"

"No! I don't know. Who are you by the way?"

"I'm Vishnu. I'm the invisible one. Also, I'm free from all blemishes. I'm perfect and everlasting bliss too. You were born out of the lotus from my navel region. You're my son." Vishnu paused for a few moments, very disturbed, Brahma began looking at Vishnu.

"Only. I'm your protector. Don't worry about anything new. None else is superior to me. I'm the master of all," said Vishnu with innocence and spontaneity.

On that angrily said Brahma, "Don't indulge in any fairy-tale. Aren't you ashamed of blowing your own trumpet and indulging shamelessly in such mean self-praise and vainglory?" Pausing briefly, he cast a sharp glance at Vishnu." In all the three worlds, I'm known as grandfather. All the four Vedas have called me Brahma. I've in one all the three attributes. Not just that much. I'm the Creator of all the three worlds too, Vishnu," said Brahma to Vishnu.

"Brahma, you're just an ignoramus. Don't be proud of anything. You aren't the creator of this universe. Only I'm the one. Only, I look after all creatures... living beings. I'm the preserver. And, only I destroy them during the dissolution of this world-pralaya. And, right now under the spell of maya, you're indulging in this self-praise!"

They could not see me. I was much amused by their that meaningless discussion. Silently, I said to myself, "How ignorant both of them are! They don't have any awareness about the real creator! What a paradox! They are both claiming to be the protector of each other."

That altercation had become very bitter. It had created a background for a lethal fight. At that very moment Shiva had reached there. Both Brahma and Vishnu had begun looking at him. His body was emitting a strange radiance. It was illuminating the entire forest with a divine light. I knew well that Shiva was fond of simplicity and humility. Very surprised by his radiant being, both, Brahma and Vishnu had become silent. In those extraordinary moments, joy coursed through my body. Both of them now tried to find out the beginning and the end point of that radiant being. So Vishnu went deep down into the earth to find out the mystery and, Brahma, flew upwards. Perhaps wrapped in their own pride, they were both unable to comprehend the truth then. For nearly one crore years, they kept searching for the provenance of that divine radiance. I was very certain that they would fail in their venture. At last, they thought of coming back, but, now they could not locate the point that they had started from. Their pride had now vanished and, now, they were eager to know about the mystery of that radiant entity. They had understood that some power was above them too. A power that was much older and superior to them. Mind enlightened, their bitterness had vanished too. The enmity within was now replaced by a feeling of devotion. Both of them now bowed before that light.

"O, you great being, all my pride has vanished now. I apologize to you I committed the mistake of considering myself the creator of this world." said Brahma with utmost humility and accepted his mistake.

"I too am an offender O radiance! please condone my indiscretion. Overcome by my vain pride, I too made the mistake of considering myself to be preserver of the world," Vishnu said with all humility and surrender.

"O! Omnipotent Being show us your true self!" pleaded Brahma to Shiva.

"O! You all powerful entity let on your identity, "Vishnu supplicated in his humblest tone.

Shiva then showed to both of them his Cosmic-Form and gave them his blessings.

After having the glimpse of that divine and Cosmic-Form of my beloved, I was now more determined to get married to him.

Those moments were very enchanting. They left an indelible impression upon my entire being. Shiva... my Rudra had given me the glimpse of that Cosmic Phallic Form. That experience cannot be put across to others at all. No words are enough to describe that. How expansive it is in form! No one can describe it with exactitude. It can only be experienced with absolute surrender. To know it through the intellect is just a grand illusion. All the Vedas have come in their manifested from only through that form. I love Shiva's that form immensely.

Time passed on....

With every passing day I was drawn closer and closer to Shiva morally and spiritually. No one could make this out. It was because I could maintain my composure. It was a complex state of mind and soul.

Meticulously, I concealed the tussle between the two diametrically opposite emotions in me. It was a painful situation. However, I did not want any disturbance at my father's place. He was a victim of a destructive pride and, I was well aware of it. There were moments when I would brood over the plight of a woman. In the solitude of my own room, I would feel how the exploitative measures were often thrust ruthlessly over a female and, how those related to her closely exploited her by referring to all those relationships. Even if she wished, she could not overlook her brothers, sisters, parents, and some other close ones.

All was crystal clear to me now. I knew well that my union with Shiva won't be an easy task. Prajapati Daksha's enmity towards Shiva had its origin in the complex psychological process. The great yogi Shiva with his long-matted hair and other strange exotic adornment was unacceptable to him. But, the real issue was something else. Prajapati Daksh felt, and we could never rise above that feeling - that Shiva had slighted Brahamadev and by torturing him had hurt his dignity.

Moreover, there was something else too. My father was a Vaishnavite in his activities and in his thoughts. He was totally ignorant of Shiva's that aughad (unconventional) form. Perhaps, he did not want to understand it either. I felt he was totally ignorant of the beauty of that lifestyle. He did not know at all the real tranquility of the relaxed modality. The beauty concealed in that could not be understood by all. But, I had been suffering silently. Teetering between doubts and suspense I, kept my grief to myself.

I cannot forget those challenging moments of my life. A woman loses the dignity of her existence, when she is forced into accepting something that she does not like at all. Prajapati had made the entire ambience spiritual in his own way. The overpowering presence of Vishnu could be felt all over that place. I cannot forget how his 'Narayan Yagya' had ended up into a fiasco. That colossal idol of Vishnu had become suddenly very heavy in those moments. All those present there were surprised and even after all efforts, the idol did not budge even a bit.

"The unveiling of the idol must be done right now. This is the most auspicious moment, " called out the saptarshis.

"Pull this float in, all of you, "Prajapati Daksha ordered his men in a loud voice. In those moments the entire atmosphere around had become festive. The people danced around and sang out spontaneously and playing on their drums began moving that huge vehicle towards the spot where it was to be placed.

"I think something has been missing about this idol, "one of the rishis pointed out.

"I don't think it is going to be a smooth affair, "said another one.

One of them let on his own opinion, "I feel if Prajapati Daksha is bent upon placing it here then what the hell are we doing here?"

All of them were eager to get away from there. They were all very perturbed in those moments.

"Let's all go away from here, one of the rishis proposed.

"You're right, "Many of them backed up the proposal in unison.

All of them got up. They looked dejected. They did not want to stay at that place even for a moment. Those were very critical moments.

Folding his hands then, Rishi Kashyap requested humbly to them, "Please listen to me with utmost attention," They had all begun looking at him. The atmosphere was tense and full of suspense. He began again, "Going away in this manner from the court of Prajapati Daksha would be discourteous.

One rishi spoke out, "But everything here is improper. Will it be according to Dharma, Kashyap?"

Kashyap then said, "Right now I have a gut feeling that whatever has been happening around here has some profound meaning. Also I feel that it's a symbol of some historic and significant activity taking place here. Let us all be a witness to that momentous happening."

All those who agreed to Kashyap's proposal, stayed back.

All efforts of taking that idol into the place assigned, failed.

It had done all of them in.

Then all the saptarishis spoke out in one voice, "Daksha, pay to us your full attention! Why don't you accept now that the very making of this idol is full of flaw? We feel that it's imperfect. In fact, any such idol cannot be set up smoothly. It seems, therefore this idol cannot be pushed to the place."

"No! I don't at all agree to your statement, "said Prajapati Daksha in a proud voice.

All of them had then become silent.

All agog and filled with surprise, I just looked on. Now, becoming tense and faces becoming full of worries, all present there definitely bewildered beyond words. The sculptor stood at one corner with his head lowered was equally confounded. He seemed to be very frightened too.

"Did you make this idol the way you were asked to do it?" I asked him.

"Yes, princess I followed the instructions to a tee," he said in a low and very uncertain voice.

"You stop worrying about anything now, sculptor! You're absolutely safe," I assured him confidently.

"Thank you, honorable princess," he said to me and, then, stopped for a few moments. He began again, "This is the first time that the idol made by me is not getting set up smoothly at the assigned place.

I'm completely flummoxed and don't know what to infer from it. Please help me out!"

Now I had understood everything. The sculptor was not to blame. He had not failed at all. The truth is that those who had ordered for it had overlooked some major point. Their fault.... failure could not be thrust upon that pure and innocent sculptor from any angle.

"Great Prajapati Daksha, you had better accept your failure and order again to have this idol completed... freed of a major fault. Once it is done it will be placed and set up where you want to have it placed, "said a rishi.

"No, great rishi, I don't agree to your suggestion." With extreme pride he then said, "I'm a perfect one. I know all rituals and their modalities. I can sort out all my problems with my own intellect. "That rishi cast a sharp glance at him. Daksha began again, "Listen to me all of you! For placing of this idol I would pray to Vishnu, the Supreme God. I'll have a yagya in his honor."

All those present there were shocked by that announcement. Those sages, scholars and great spiritual luminaries were at a loss and did not know how to react on to that meaningless utterance. One could see on those faces a profound anxiety. The whole atmosphere around the place had become very tense. A silence had spread over there too. Moments passed. They kept looking at one another.

At last, breaking that long silence, one of those learned sages spoke out, "What, Prajapati Daksha! What sort of an announcement is this? How could you do this?"

Then, overcome by his own pride, my father said, "Tell me only one thing!" The sage looked at Prajapati. "What's your problem, O learned sage! Right now, you're my guest and my invitee. You don't have to criticize me. Just stand by my decision. It'll bring you greater regards... Do you catch on?"

Shocked greatly, the sage just looked at Prajapati. All present these at that moment, maintained a discreet silence. "It feels that you don't know at all what the Narayan Yagya is all about," said he with pauses.

"Ha! Don't teach me like that. My dear reverend sir, I know all about the yagya. And here, you're bent on insulting your Prajapati in this manner! It's disgusting! Just do what you're supposed to do. It'll bring you respect, "said Prajapati.

"No - Prajapati, this isn't very convincing. I mean your statement! If you had known it properly then, it wouldn't have come into your mind at all. In my view, the very idea of this yagya is disastrous," said one another sage in a high tone.

Daksha cast a sharp glance at the speaker. Sounding annoyed and hurt, he said in a strident voice, "I don't appreciate this unnecessary interference. It'll just create unpleasantness."

On that one more sage said, with a view to reducing tension, "Prajapati Daksha, listen to me attentively." My father looked at him sharply. He went on, "Great Prajapati, I look up to you. You excel all others here in management skill. All systems here run smoothly, only because of you. In my opinion you're a pragmatic philosopher, and, yet, I feel that you must pay attention to the advice that you're being suggested to at the moment." Briefly, he paused. His face was extremely grave. All others have been looking at him closely. He began again. "Naraya Yagya is a complex one. For it, you have to get water from several rivers. You have to arrange 108 types of flowers too for it. But, Parijat flowers must be there." He stopped, fixing his sharp gage upon Daksha. The silence at the place had thickened Prajapati Daksha had an indifferent look on his countenance. "Where are you going to get all those Parijat flowers from, Prajapati? asked the sage.

My father, Prajapati Daksha burst into laughter. Proud and confident, he said, "Dear sir, perhaps, you've forgotten at this moment who you have been talking to. And, don't even forget about my resourcefulness. Now, here I give you my advice." All those present there began looking at my father. "Now, gentlemen put aside all your meaningless worries, and start planning for the yagya. I'm determined to perform this Narayan Yagya. Let it be known to all."

While it was all going on, I saw an opportunity of pleasing the father. I said, “Father, I'll arrange the Parijat flowers.” I paused. He looked at me, his eyes shining. “I don't have doubts about it. I can do it. I have full faith in me” I added.

On hearing me, he was greatly amused. “Sati, this isn't a game for kids,” he said, his face spread out in a smile. I looked at him. His eyes were glowing with love. It was all reflected in the expression of his face.” How tender, you're my child! Parijat flowers are only found in deep and dense forest. Reaching there is an extremely complex and difficult task. You aren't even just aware of the difficulties on the way, “he added and kept quiet. A silence ensued I kept looking at him and tried to guess his thoughts. Closely observing my face, he began again, “I can't cause any bothers to my darling girl, just for the fulfillment of my vow.”

On that I said, “After all, I'm your daughter!”

“What do you want to tell me, Sati?”

“Am I less obdurate than you?”

“But, at certain occasions, obduracy isn't the best option,” he said in a grave tone and rather philosophically.

“Don't worry about me, father,” I said in a steady tone.

Further, he spoke out, “Should I send you all alone in that deserted place Sati?”

To assure him I said, "Just give your blessings," He looked at me, his eyes had a troubled look. "My sisters will accompany me too. Together, we're capable of facing any challenge, "I told him. He did not speak out anything immediately. A smile came over my face. "After all, we're all the daughters of, great, renowned Prajapati Daksha."

My statement delighted him. He kept looking at me, his eyes brimming over with love.

"Sati!" he called out after a long pause."

"Tell me, Prajapati. What's your final decision?"

He laughed. I knew instantly that he was very happy. He could never hold his emotions in. His face was completely transparent.

After a long silence, he said, "Sati, you're a headstrong child! You always act on your whims."

I smiled and, then said, "Only you're to blame for that."

"How do you blame me for that?

"You always fulfill my demand, and I'm very sure, that is the reason for my being so stubborn," I said and tried to read the expression of his face.

"So, my dear girl, you have been brazenly suggesting that I made a mistake by giving you all that freedom! You want to suggest that I failed as a parent. I don't know how to react to that!" he said in a slightly louder voice.

In those moments - and, I could guess it clearly– that his voice was moist with very tender emotions.

Driven on by strong emotions, I felt a thrill of pleasure coursing through my body then, I said with pauses, "My dear father, I'm grateful to you for all that immense love that you've showered upon me without any miserliness. Your love and trust for me has been the greatest prop in my life."

His eyes moistened. Perhaps, it had set forth a chain of strong emotions in him too. He just kept looking at me intently. His eyes glowing, he said, breaking a long pause, "Sati, now you go and get those flowers with the help of your sisters. This is the most urgent task before you at this moment."

We had gone to the forest.... we had to collect 108 kinds of flowers. We had begun collecting them. All alone, I had walked towards a pond. Then, I had seen a strange object in the middle of a lotus flower. My sisters had given me idea about a rudraksha. That object resembled a rudraksha. Silently, I picked it up and moved up further from there.

Suddenly, I started and stopped. A beautiful vista was lying before me. Beyond the valley were hillocks. In the middle of them on the top was a big, black statue in the phallic shape. I felt a strange sensation in my body at those moments. I felt then as if a divine and exotic delicacy... softness was growing within me. I know... felt that I was different from all others... completely different. For a few moments, I became totally oblivious of my own presence and, the existence of my sisters. A huge awareness seemed to have been rising within me too. I looked intently before me. All of a sudden, I had a strange experience. Often when we are in a standing position then our shadow seem to be similar... identical with what we are in actuality. But, in the shadow of that phallic rock, I saw a male form. He had the look of a yogi. The shadow had long, matted locks. He had a trident in his hand. And, when I kept looking at it... the shadow... it had vanished into the thin air... the void.

I kept on walking. As soon as crossed that valley, I saw a few caves in the woods. A number of sages were sitting there. Some of them were lost in their own meditation, and some others were busy in paying their obeisance to damru and trident. I felt .... experienced a unique and profound tranquility in those moments. As soon as they became aware of my presence, quickly all of them got up and greeted me with folded hands.

Overcome by extreme surprise, I asked them, "O reverent sages, putting aside your meditation and pooja, why have you all been greeting me with such reverence?"

On that one of them came forward and said with extreme love and reverence, "You're welcome to sage Dadhichi's ashram!"

Greeting them too with my folded hands, I said, "I've lost my way and have reached, this place. Please show me the way!"

"Only after losing your way, will you find your way," called out someone from behind.

I looked back. Only the sage Dadhichi was coming towards me. He had layers of ashes all over his body. A rudraksha mala was around his neck. Even on his matted locks, he had put on a mala. His bright and shining face had a soft and charming smile.

"Daughter, don't be surprised on seeing all these sadhus with ashes all over their bodies" he said humorously.

My courtesy and humility impressed him a lot. He said "Daughter, this ash is the ultimate truth of life. It keeps us aware of the ephemeral nature of our life all the time. Only it can ensure our, liberation from the bondage of this physical world. It alone can have us freed from the clutches of ignorance." He paused for a few moments and, began brooding over something. Quietly, I kept looking at him. Then, pointing towards his rudraksha mala, he began saying, "Sati.... my daughter, these're the rudraksha seeds. These are a source of vitality.... life and never wither at all. In fact, these're like a soul. At every moment of our life, we keep this truth of life with us. These keep us, all the time, conscious of a divinity." He pauses for a few moments again. After a long gap, he began again, his tone very grave, "The truth is that this rudraksha mala is the real identity of a true Shiva bhakta."

"Shiva bhakt!" I asked, incredulous.

On that sage Dadhichi said, "Yes, devi Sati, all of us here are Shiva bhakts. Only Shiva is the Creator of this entire universe. He is the Preserver of it all too. He alone is the Destroyer of evil ones. The whole world reveres him and pays obeisance to him. But, only your father, Prajapati Daksha, is his opponent. Only, he harbors enmity against the great Lord."

I did not want to be a sinner by listening to my father's criticism by someone. By I knew it at the heart of my hearts that whatever is being said by sage Dadhichi then was not at all questionable. It was a very complex situation for me. I was bound by my filial duties. In those moments I was thinking how difficult it was for someone to get over the harrowing doubts when one is faced with the questions of morality. It is very difficult to make up one's mind on such occasions. So, the best thing then seemed to me to keep quiet and change the topic.

I said to sage Dadhichi, "I must go away from here now. My sisters must be worrying about me a lot. I've lost the way and, they must be overcome by concern about me. Now if I don't reach there soon, they'd infer that I'm in some trouble."

But, I was extremely surprised when the sage Dadhichi told me, "Devi, the parijat flowers that you have been looking for, will be available only here."

Greatly surprised, I could only utter, "Is it possible!"

"This is the truth, Devi! Come along with me into the forest."

"Dear sir, I want to ask you something," I said, curious.

"Ask that Sati!"

"Was my coming to this place predestined?"

He began laughing. When I began looking at him, he said, "What's hidden from Lord Shiva? Daughter, he knows everything!"

"So, the setting up of that idol at the temple must be prefixed too?" I asked him.

His tone was extremely serious when he said, "Devi Sati that idol will reach the temple is predetermined too. Even the Narayan Yagya conceived by your great father', Prajapati Daksha."

"Why is it so, reverend sir?" I asked, my voice having a trace of pain.

"This is all the will of that absolute power."

"Can it be neutralized?"

"No!"

He took me along with him to a place where a huge rock in Phallic Form was located. It was so near to me that I could have touched it. The sanctity of the place had great attraction. I had forgotten my real state of mind. For a few seconds, I was drawn into the sight before me. In those moments, it seemed to have contained me. Overcome by pleasure, I was transported into a different world. I felt as if I was only an inseparable part of that Phallic Form.

I came back to my own self when, the deep voice of sage Dadhichi floated into my ears, "Close your eyes, Sati try to visualize the idol of Narayan that has been built up by your father's order. Once you do it, you'll come to find out why it's imperfect. What's missing in it?

With curiosity and astonishment, I moved forward. The desire for finding the truth about it had become very intense in me. It had been impelling me constantly and, now, the impulse had become unbearable. Inadvertently, my hand touched the stone. I felt as if lightning had flashed before me. I felt a shiver running down from head to foot. Those divine moments had seeped through my entire being. That was the emanation from a comprehensive and omnipotent consciousness. The energy flowing out from it, after entering my being, was transforming my whole self. It was now full of Shiva's presence. I had now fully understood the flaw in my father's devotion. He was unable to understand that no other god's presence could be visualized without the presence of Shiva.

❑

At several occasions my father, Prajapati Daksha, would assume himself to be the director of everything. He thought that his own way of doing the things was the best one. Only his system in the world was without any fault. Also he thought, he was totally convinced that his system... and style of working could give perfection to the functioning of the world. He would say it before sages and savants and spiritual luminaries whenever he got a chance for it. It was his big passion. His own self-praise annoyed others a lot. There were even moments when I would feel that his pride and self-praise bedimmed his mind. He was totally unaware that Vishnu himself was a devotee of Shiva. He had no idea that Vishnu could not enter a place where Shiva was not given proper respect. His Daksha Samhita is an expression of his nescience. Here, Daksha has tried to mention that in his opinion Shiva is not a God at all. At least he does not take him for God. It is Prajapati's conviction that the very presence of Shiva pollutes the ambience.

How great is my Lord Shiva! From time to time, he has not just taken the test of the human beings: he has even taken the test of gods too. Even Vishnu is not unaware of it. He knows well that Shiva bhakt cannot be killed without the will of Shiva himself. Many demons have been bhakts of Shiva too. Once Vishnu thought of killing the Shiva bhakt demons, so he could protect the people from the oppressions and cruelties of the demons. And, while doing so, he would wipe out the forces of darkness. It would reduce the load on the earth too. Vishnu then went to Shiva's abode-Kailash. Every day, he would chant mantras in praise of Shiva. He recited Shiva's name a thousand times every day. He even offered a thousand lotus flowers at Shiva-ling. Acting like a child, Shiva indulged in prank, and made one lotus flower disappear from the lot of those thousand lotus flowers.

Finding one lotus flower missing, Vishnu looked for it all around. However, after failing in finding that missing lotus flower, he gouged out one of his eyes that resembles a lotus flower, and, offered that to lord Shiva. Once, Shiva himself had called Vishnu lotus-eyed. At that time with a very lethal weapon, Vishnu had destroyed and killed all those Shiva bhakt demons.

At one occasion, when Prajapati, my father, was boasting about his own powers and, in that mood, even insulted learned sages; at that time Shiva ......

reminded Prajapati Daksha about his rights and about his limits.

I still remember what Shiva had said about him then. "I'm not attached to the world. I'm above honor and insults. In this world, neither does anyone belong to me nor do I belong to any one either. I've got nothing to do with anyone. I'm above all desires... longing. Enjoyment of the worldly pleasures doesn't have any place in my life. I feel it only makes one selfish. It blurs only his moral vision. Also it makes him full of uncertainty when he is faced with some ethical and moral issue. Only a detached soul can take the right moral judgment. A relentless pursuit of gross worldly pleasures stains one's righteous character. I've an abiding faith in dharma. It's my conviction that it alone can give one stability and transparency. What's this dharam after all? This is a divine consciousness. It is, in my view, a spiritual expansion of a human being However, when it falls into vanity and, becomes an outward show off, then even one's upright conduct is changed into a wrong one. I must also tell you here too that when it begins encouraging and backing up prejudice and discrimination and all others evil proclivities, then I am forced to step in and destroy the evil."

Maybe, my father took that for his insult. Without uttering a single word, he got up and walked away from that place. With him all others had gone away too. I was left all alone in that expansive temple.

The idol had been placed in the temple. I was extremely happy then. But, at the same time, I experience a feeling of dejection too. I felt as if my father was very upset with my conduct. Perhaps, in those moment he felt that the daughter he loved most, had let him down before others. I was very pained by that. It was a complex mental state. I was torn by the opposite pulls of different kinds of emotions. A sense of deep vacancy was slowly but certainly gripping my thought process. I now intensely longed to get back into the secure solitude of my own room. But, I did not know then how I would face all others comfortably. In those moments, I just kept thinking about resentment of my mother, anger of my father and frustration of my sisters. I kept thinking over my plight for a long time. Finally, I decided go back into my own chamber. I walked towards that. Khyati didi stopped me on the way. She sounded quite indignant when she said, “What do you think yourself to be, Sati?” I cast a sharp and question glance at her.” Our father loves you most! And what have you given him in return?”

In a low tone, I mumbled, “Didi, please make it clear to me.”

She burst out, “Now don’t act as if you don’t know what I have been referring to, Sati. You aren’t a small and innocent girl... You’re a mature one.

I said, “No-didi, don’t say all those things to me. Your words have hurt me deeply. Believe me, I’m unable to grasp what you have been hinting at!”

After hearing my words, angrily she began shouting, “Don’t overstrain father’s love. It has well-defined limits. You enjoy great latitude, but, it doesn’t give you a right to do whatever you want to!”

“What’s its significance in the present context, didi?” I asked in a slightly louder voice. She looked at me, “At least, the reference must be clear to me too!”

“You made father feel small before others today!” she shouted.

“How did I do it? You can’t justify your statement,” I said with a hint of firmness in my voice.

“Without father’s permission, you set up at the temple that symbol of Shiva!”

I laughed, “You’re angry over only at this paltry issue, aren’t you?”

“Is it a small issue?” she asked.

“Is it a big issue then?”

“Yes it is, Sati.”

“How?”

“Any slight of father is an unpardonable offence, “said she, hissing.”

I explained, “If I hadn’t done that then that idol couldn’t have been set up there at all.” I paused and tried to read... guess her thoughts. Her face was livid with rage. At last, breaking that long silence, I said, “If I hadn’t done that then, I feel, it would have embarrassed him terribly before others. To save him from that only, I set up that Shiva's symbol there."

After hearing that, she lost control over her. Her voice rose, she said, "I feel, you went against his basic philosophy of life. You made him an object of laughter before others. All those present there must have been laughing at his back. In some way his status has been reduced before others. Your action must have hurt him deeply. In my opinion, today, he has lost his dignity!"

I said to Khyati didi, "I'm exceedingly pained by your words... utterance. You have been unkind towards me! I never meant it to be interpreted in your way! What could be more pitiful than the situation when your own people begin questioning and doubting your own intentions?"

"You have been just talking about your own pain! Selfish! You don't seem to have perceptivity to make out how others have been hurt and pained by your own actions." said she in a very harsh tone.

... All my sisters were sad about the incident. My mother too seemed to be deeply hurt. I felt a profound alienation in the midst of them. Shocked and shattered, I was within, but no one present there was sensitive enough to listen to me and commiserate with me. No one was there to reason and show me a way out. I did not myself even have enough courage to face the father now. The way he had turned at the temple ceremony and stamped out of there, had punctured my courage and boldness completely. ... I was musing over that family impasse. It seemed to me in those moments that all of us there were then nonplussed. I seemed to have been caught up in the worst dilemma. Suddenly, an idea flashed across my mind. It relaxed me. I felt that only my dear Lord Shiva would help me out from that imbroglio. I don't know when I had given myself away totally to him. I was driven on by the most impelling love. It existed in a microscopic form. And, it could not be seen with the physical eyes at all.... The moment I thought of my Shiva... my Rudra, I experienced a profound peace within me. Even in that vast mental darkness, I had seen a faint light. Those were the most precious moments. I stood before the mirror. My dull countenance was once more beaming.

I came out my room. And, then walking slowly, I had reached my mother's room.

"Who is there?" my mother called out, after hearing the sound of my footsteps.

"It's me... Sati," I said in a ten voice.

"Yes- Sati! What do you want, my dear?"

"Mother, I want to talk to you."

"Come on in, Sati."

I went in.

"What do you want to tell me now?

"I want to discuss something with you," I said in a low tone.

Her face darkened and her eyes narrowed. "What's there now to discuss, daughter?'

"Do you feel hurt?" I asked, looking deeply into her eyes.

"What's the use of brooding over any unpleasantness", she said philosophically.

"Even then!"

"In my book of life there aren't ifs and buts, my daughter."

"Have I hurt you?"

"Very much."

"Why do you ask it now, Sati?" She paused. I tried to guess her thoughts. Her face was opaque. "What's gone is gone forever", she said in a neutral tone.

"Can it be nullified now?"

"I don't know." She stopped. "Do you have something on your mind?"

I threw my arms round her neck. A shiver ran down her body. I could feel it. My spirit perked up. I said to explain my point, "It was all instinctive, mother. I did it in good will. The truth is something had a hold over me in those moments. I didn't know what had been impelling me to act on like that then. Don't overlook it now. It'll be tragic. It will destroy me!"

Mother looked at me. Embracing each other, we had begun weeping. First slowly, then loudly.

“Calm down now, my darling”, said my mother to console me.

I stopped. Then, looking at her, I asked with a smile, “And what about you?” Tenderly embracing me, she said, her voice was rich with the emotion of love, “What should we do now?” I looked at her. She explained, “We must restore the peace in this house.”

An idea flashed across my mind. I observed her face. She was not very sure of herself. “Please take me to father,” I said to her.

“Will it be all right, Sati.”

“This is the best course of action in these moments,” I told her. I paused, brooding over the situation. “It’ll break the ice,” I added.

She could know how disturbed I was. Gently, she passed her fingers through my hair. Her that intimate touch had all sweetness. I cannot express it in words. However, it consoled me greatly.

My mother then told me, her mind made up, “Okay- dear Sati! I feel that right now, only you can calm down the disturbed Prajapati. Come along with me.”

We walked towards the room where he would brood over his own problems. His face looked dull. I could make out that he was very disturbed and unhappy. We had stood before him. He looked questioningly at my mother.

“Sati wants to tell you something,” she blurted out.

"What else is left there now?" he muttered blankly.

"Please, just listen to her, dear husband," said mother in a pleading voice. Father looked at her. Give her a chance to explain everything. She loves you!

I observed his face and all those emotions that just kept flashing across his countenance then. I knew that he could not conceal his feelings. They would appear on his face. I also knew that a little acceptance of my own mistake would thaw his angry feelings.

"Father!" I could utter with great effort.

"Yes, my dear one? Tell me whatever you want to! I love you!"

Slowly, but with the utmost clarity, I said, "Because of me, your dignity was lowered before others today." I could not utter anything further.

His fair and broad forehead had begun beaming once more with the awareness of his own status and authority. It had pleased me immensely.

"I have been an offender," I said in a low tone.

"I don't accept it," he said.

"Will you forgive me?"

"Sati!"

"Yes, father?"

"I want to tell you something now."

"Please tell me whatever is on your mind."

Then, he said, his voice stable, "We must always think about our present. That's the most important thing. Do you know why?"

"Why?" I asked.

He went on, "Because the very foundation of our future depends on it. Brooding over the past is a waste of time and resources. It doesn't help us at all. The truth is that it even destroys our present." He paused briefly and began to look at us. I saw that my mother was looking at him appreciatively. "Even you too forget what you said and did in the past. Get over your unhappiness now," he said to me.

My mother and father were very happy then. Mainly my mother was very pleased with my confession.

Only in those moments did I realize that what mattered most in a society is the family happiness. The bitter truth is when parents are slighted and looked down upon by their own children, and then they are shattered grievously. They are lost and overpowered by a feeling of inferiority. All their dignity lost, they become indifferent to all pleasures and activities of life. In those moments I realized too that I had to fulfill my own duties towards my parents.

"Father!" I mumbled out.

"Yes, my dear one, what has put you out so much? Won't you share it with your own father?"

Gazing at him, I said, “I want to expiate for my own offence.”

“What to expiate! What offence have you been referring to, Sati?”

“For causing you pain.”

“But, no longer am I unhappy.”

“But you were earlier!”

“Don’t brood over that now, Sati.”

“I’m helpless against that.”

“But you must make efforts to get over it. Continued blues is detrimental to your health.”

“Father, I’ve a request to make.”

“Why is this hesitation before your own father, Sati? What do you want to tell me?”

“You must decide some punishment for me.”

“Why do you want a punishment for you?”

“Because I’ve failed in fulfilling the duties of a daughter.”

“But I’ve already forgiven youhave granted you a pardon.”

On that I muttered, “I want to tell something else too.”

He laughed. “Get over your emotions and then, think over this issue from a different angle, daughter.”

I almost wept when I said, “Father, you’re Prajapati Daksha. You’re the director of the world.

Your justice isn't governed by emotions. It's related to a moral duty and is limited by it too."

My father cut in, "Daughter, state clearly what do you want from me?"

"Father, just announce your punishment. That's what I want from you right now."

"But I've already condoned you, daughter."

"I haven't been looking for any relaxation."

"What do you want then?"

"Punishment!"

"I can't give you that."

"Why can't you?" I asked, challenging him.

"A king is not bound by anything. Everything depends on his discretion. His will matters most. The truth is that only a completely free person can be a king," said loudly my father.

"No – Father! You're wrong on this issue. I don't agree to your view. You don't have absolute freedom either."

"How do you vindicate your statement ... observation?"

"I can do so by reminding you of your commitment as a king."

"My commitment as a king?"

"Yes, that's the thing!"

"How do you define it?"

"Justice must be separated from emotions and feelings. A king ought to be aware of it all the time. This is his commitment.

"Sati!"

"Yes, father!"

"Don't you want any forgiveness?"

"No!"

"Okay – then you ought to be punished!"

"I'll willingly accept any punishment, Prajapati!"

"But what offence should you be punished for?"

"I'll clear up..."

"Do so."

"I don't want to be punished for setting up the Shiva-ling at the temple. I don't have to conceal my love for Shiva any more. But, I've definitely committed and unpardonable offence by going against the will of my father. I hurt his dignity is the general perception here. I now want to atone for that.

On hearing that, my father spoke out, "Dear daughter, I catch it on now. I assure you that you're sure to get a punishment." Briefly pausing after that, he added, "I've already decided a punishment for you."

I said, "Whatever it is, I'll accept it gracefully."

My father had bowed down before my insistence. While announcing his verdict, he said, "Sati as punishment for seven days, you won't eat anything." Prajapat Daksha, the judge, paused for a few moments and began brooding over something. Time passed. Then, looking around, he began saying in a grave voice, "Also, you'll have to write the name of Lord Vishnu in one lakh leaves of the Lotus flower." He stopped again. Then, fixing his gaze upon me, he went on, "One thing more, I point out categorically here again that you'll have to wipe out the very image and memory of Shiva, from your mind. Your contact with that aghori Shiva is totally banned at this place."

That cruel and unfeeling announcement had put me out. My face had become impassive afterwards. In the heart of hearts, I knew that it was just a part of my dear one's leela. I had also made up my mind to carry out my father's will till the end. My aim was to abide by his words with the utmost devotion. It was totally a filial commitment. Perhaps, Shiva wished that, in no case, the peace of the family be disturbed. In the depths of my heart, I could know that it was the purest form of love at its best. It had touched me to the core.

Love, in itself, is a form of yagya. Those who have perceived its infinite expanse, rise above the gross materialism of the world. They experience a surge of energy in them. It courses though their entire being. Once it is experienced, they are elevated to a higher world of spiritual existence. They are purged of violence and enmity. Very few of us are aware of the fact that love has the power of purifying man's self. I came to know how love, at some level, a form of renunciation and abstinence. It is a self-sufficient, sui generis object. It is a vast and extremely alluring proposition. Love is the great and the most reliable prop. With it one can win any opposition or face any difficulty.

I had no delusion about the entire thing. All formalities, and course of activities of the penance had been chalked out and determined. I had no doubts left in me. The only consideration before me now was the successful completion of the penance. I did not experience any pain either. My equanimity had reached new heights.

Clearing up mother's doubts, I told her, my voice assuring, "Mother, I'm the daughter of Prajapati Daksha. Now give up your worries about me. I'll pass the test. I trust my own abilities. I can take on this punishment comfortably and put up with the hardships.

My mother was a tender female. She did not take my words for granted. She said, her eyes full of uncertainty," How will you live for seven days without my food, daughter. I'll request your father to reduce the severity of punishment by allowing some relaxation.

I told my mother then, "Don't even try it, mother! He has a though knowledge of justice: what is right or what is wrong. He knows well what punishment is to be meted out to an offender, the violator of law. He's legality. Looking for any extenuation in the matter, would be our doubting his judgment."

My logic appealed to my mother. She said, "Sati, I appreciate your discretion and your perspicacity. I'm immensely proud of your being my daughter. You've glorified my life." She paused for a few moments. She cast a loving glance at me. It gave me lots of pleasure. Then, she said, her voice very tender and mellifluous, "You have always been very conscious of dharma Sati. I give you my countless blessings."

My mother Prasuti was the daughter of Manu and Shatrupa. She had a very radiant and noble personality. She was an ideal and virtuous wife. She followed Prajapati Daksha in every way. She never questioned his decisions. They were both a foil to each other. My father had a mercurial temper, but, in contrast to that, mother had a calm and patient nature. My father had a streak of pride too, but, mother was a very image of humility. Notwithstanding such profound contrast in characters, they had a very successful married life."

...One of the shaptarishis, sage Bhrigu was my brother brother-in-law. He was the founder of astrology. He could have fore knowledge of the coming events through astrology. He had perceived beforehand the course of events of my future life. He was now much worried about my wellbeing. He had been trying best for countervailing the evil effects and possibilities of the horoscope with some other measures that could propitiate the malefic forces. It was because his own loyalty was towards his father-in-law, Prajapati Daksha.

...My penancepunishment was about to start. My sisters wanted to fulfill their duties by assisting and helping me. I was reluctant to take their help. My mother wished that I should take the assistance of all my sisters for collecting those flowers. But, the idea did not appeal to me at all, and, I resisted it. my mother and sisters had fully understood by now that I wouldn't accept their suggestion. They were fully aware of my headstrong character. Even then, they were all very worried about memy well-being. They kept pleading to me. It did not have any effect upon me.

At last, I said, looking at them fixedly, "I request all of you to pay attention to me. All your these words aren't going to make me change my mind. I'll collect all the lotus flower leaves myself." I paused for a few moments. They looked at me desperately. I raised my voice. "Now I don't want to discuss anything with you. It's a settled issueNo more discussions over it," I added in one breath.

My words had disturbed my mother a lot. In a low and painful voice, she said, "Sati, I've just been thinking about your problems and troubles. To think about all that makes me nervous."

Those were the sweetest moments. They were a symbol of an ideal family tradition where all members of the family thought about one another. How beautiful is the atmosphere of families whose elders have unconditional love for their younger ones and look after their needs and try to fulfill them to the best possible extent. And a place where the younger members of the family look up to the senior ones and pay them all regards and where the junior ones abide by the commands and directions of the senior members.

I kept brooding over all kinds of things.

I did not have much idea then about handling the thing. Gazing at my mother fixedly, I said, "Don't weaken my determination by giving me any order now. I love you most in the world." I paused to recollect my thoughts. My mother had been looking at me. My voice moistened when I said, "Your complete faith in me is the base of my life. Now, I request you not to break it up."

I tried my best to calm her down.

Penance was about to start. Determined, I came out my room. I was completely calm and steady. Perhaps, my own will power was responsible for it. Standing outside, my sisters had been waiting for me. I had liked all that in those moments. I felt a fresh surge of energy then.

"Sati, let's go out to collect the flowers," proposed Rohini Didi.

Many other attendants were lined up there too.

"What's all this about?" I asked, looking at my sisters.

"Why? Don't we have to collect flowers?" asked Aditi didi authoritatively.

But, I have to carry out this task all alone! Why are you all here? I don't understand!" I said, somewhat bitterly.

"You're a headstrong kind, Sati," said Rohini Didi, rebuking me.

"How?"

"What's the problem if we accompany you?" Aditi didi asked me, her voice angry.

"Won't it reduce the gravity and importance of my penance?"

"No – not at all!" said Rohini Didi.

"Why not?" I asked, annoyed.

"Because, we're all one," said Aditi didi.

"But our karmic activities are individualistic, aren't they? Aren't they private and personal?" I paused. They looked at me. "The effects of our karmas?"

Their faces had dulled. They had begun looking at one another. They did not know how to counter my agreement. They were at sixes and sevens.

Breaking that embarrassing silence, Khyati didi said, "What sort of obduracy is this, Sati? First you demanded punishment from our father. Now you're being stubborn about this issue of collecting the lotus-flower leavesI'm much confused and frustrated!"

Then said, Rohini didi, "What is the time at your disposal? Just a week only!" Then, pausing briefly, she cast a sharp glance at me. "How would you manage to collect that number of flowers when you're on this severe fast?"

While these discussions were going on, our mother had reached. She had heard all those takes. Defending my viewpoint, she said, "Sati is right. This is the result of her own Karma and, she must go through it by herself. She fell silent for a few moments. However, a silent suffering had clearly on her countenance. Then, breaking a long and painful silence, she began again, "And, don't even forget for a moment that she's the daughter of Prajapati Daksha. She'll carry out this penance all alone. We should only pray for her safety. I'm certain about her success".

Without having any food, I had come out the palace barefooted with two attendants, without even taking any water, I had been facing the scorching sun. only the power of my determination had been driving me on in those moments. I did not want it to get slackened. In those moments, my heart was filled with reverence for our father's awareness of Dharma and his commitment to Justice. Only because of these qualities in his characters, he had not backed out from meting out harsh punishment to a tender and delicate princess of the palace. What glorious magnitude had that awareness and wisdom of Dharma! It compelled even a princess to step out all alone from the palace for attaining her goal.

To help me in my mission, my sisters had the flowers from nearby places collected by the maids of the palace. Perhaps, God did not wish me to get them easily. To get them now, I had moved on further. I could not get them in ponds and other water bodies. The evening was approaching fast. My maids were all in by now. They began requesting me to return. I sent them back and moved ahead in search of the lotus flowers.

The sculptors had been brought to the court of my father. Prajapati now wanted to punish them for something that they were not at all responsible. It was context of that idol of Vishnu. Prajapati Daksha held them responsible for everything. They pleaded innocence. However, my father had banished them from his land. It was a very tragic moment; but, it had no effect on Prajapati. In his view, those sculptors had committed an unpardonable offence. They were being meted out a condign punishment. It was justice at its best. It could not be questioned. Nor could it be rescinded either.

While it was going on, sage Dadhichi had reached there with some other sages. They had begun chanting loudly in praise of Shiva.... It had enraged Prajapati Daksha.

"What have you been doing it for, o venerated sage? It doesn't become you to act so irresponsibly. You have been violating the ethical code and hurting my dignity too! I can't put up with this gross infringement of discipline here! Please stop all this immediately. This is my order! I rule this place."

"No! Not at all!" blurted out the sage. Then, casting a searing glance at Prajapati, he said intrepidly," O Ignorant ruler-Prajapati Daksha, what could be above Mahadevi?"

"Stop it right now! I cannot accept this nonsense anymore!" shouted loudly my father at the sage. He paused for a few moments, groping for more insulting words. The sage kept looking at him. He began again, "You haven't been invited to this place. You're an unwanted person."

Dadhichi, the sage and all other sages accompanying him, had gone away from there. I was not present there but, it was narrated by Rohini didi to me. It had pained me a lot.

"Don't you have any other thing to do?" my father had asked says Dadhichi. He paused for a few moments, before he said, his voice full of sarcasm, "I know the secret!"

"What's the secret, Prajapati?"

"You Shiva bhakstsdevotees have no other job to do. You just fritter away your time and energy on such meaningless activities. No one invites the devotees of Shiva to sacred functions now! I know it well!" He stopped and stared at the sage. In those moments Dadhichi's eyes were glowing with anger. My father began again, "Everything is transparent now. It seems because of aghori Shiva's company, all his devotees have become shameless and have lost their sense of self-respect. Uninvited, they gatecrash at any place and expect all kinds of hospitality. They've lost the sense of etiquetteI'm surprised at this audacity!"

Sage Dadhichi maintained his cool. Without any feeling of hurt, he asked, "Why do you punish these innocent sculptors, Prajapati?"

"I'm not obliged to give you any explanation", said Prajapati. He cast a sharp glance at the erudite sags. "How does it matter to you?" he asked the sages.

"It matters."

"How? Are you a king or a judge?"

"I'm not."

"Then?"

The sage said, his voice loud and clear, "Wherever some helpless person is victimized, a devotee of Shiva doesn't have to wait for any invitation then. I've come to you with that authority only."

Overcome by uncontrollable rage now, my father shouted, "Don't compel me to forget my etiquettes. I see you're incorrigible! Right now, go away from this place, lest I should commit some moral and social offence.

Overlooking Prajapati's warning, sage Dadhnichi said, his voice firm, "O great Prajapati Daksha, these sculptors aren't the offenders from any angle."

"I'm not bound to explain my action to you."

"But, I'm bent upon finding it out."

"Prjapati Daksha is the supreme authorityHe's free and above all laws," "said my father with pride in his voice.

"This is nothing but sheer megalomania!"

"No ruler can attain glory by making his people angry and dissatisfied," said the wise sage in an even voice.

"Stop your voice sermon, Dadhichi!"

"This isn't a sermon!"

"It is."

"No – it isn't."

"I hold steadfast to my statement", said Prajapati.

On that sage Dadhichi said, "Don't be a headstrong person, Prajapati. Power is a deceptive thing. When it overpowers a person, he's then sure to fall into darkness and swallowed by it."

For a few moments, Prajapati Daksha could not speak anything. Then after a brief deliberation, he said, rather sardonically, "I feel, mostly the devotees of Shiva are undisciplined and anarchical.

They indulge in abnormal practices. They're totally devoid of good manners." Briefly he paused and tried to organize his thoughts. "If I can punish my own daughter for her violation of rules and law, the, I can punish anyone else too for the same," he said and paused. "Since the punishment has already been announced for these sculptors, a withdrawal isn't at all possible. These fellows will have to go through it now. I request you stop interfering in the matter."

On that, sage Dadhichi "said All right – o great Prajapati! From today, I'll give them shelter. But, never ever forget that someday you might lose your all people!

"What do you want to tell me now?"

"You might be left all alone."

At that very moment, my father announced, "Anyone who doesn't want to abide by rules and regulations of this place, is free to go away with these aghoris."

"All of us want to stay with you only Prajapati," said loudly all of them in unison.

A smile flashed across rage Dadhichi's face. Fixing his gaze upon Prajapati Daksha, he said, his eyes glowing with amusement, "You're a very popular figureking, Prajapati! Congrats!"

Playing his damru and uttering and chanting loudly 'Har..Har Mhadeva'--- he went away from there with his pupils. I had come back to the place with the load of those lotus flowers on my shoulder. I had searched through the forest all alone. My soles were bleeding profusely and hurting. That strain had done me in. At that time, my mission was the most important thing for me. So, I was just oblivious of my physical hurts and pains. But, the moment, I entered my own room, thirst and hunger had attacked me at once. The walls and all articles of decor seemed to have been reeling before me. My head was swimming and, I felt, as if I was getting swallowed into a powerful flux of nothingness. There seemed to be a circular motion around me. Its spread frightened me. I could not make out what power was there that had been directing all that, Just before me appeared the image of my dear one with his damru and trisul. Using my utmost will-power, I dispelled that image from my mind and, thus, I abided by the promise that I had given to my father. In those moments I thought if a woman was at all free in the world. How difficult it was for her to turn her back on her own love and give it up! How cruel and apathetic this society was that thrust upon all sorts of demands upon her! It forces her into submission. Her tender feelings have no valueimportance before the expectations of a hidebound society. She is a fettered being. She is not given any option. She is a slave at some level. I was extremely tired. Brooding over all that, I passed out.

❑

When I came to, my mother and all my sisters and my attending maids were all around me. They looked worried. In those moments, I experienced a strange joy over powering me. Their concern for me was surprisingly refreshing. Their silent but profound love was all reflected in their eyes.

"How're you now, Sati?" my mother asked.

"You don't pay much attention to your wellbeing," said Aditi didi. Then, bending over me, she gently passed her one hand over my head. Softly, she kissed my forehead. "Okay- now, I'll help you sit up! We're burning with curiosity at this moment. Tell us about your adventure."

"Stop doing that Aditi!" entering my room, called out our father in a loud voice.

Shocked, Aditi didi began looking at Prajapati Daksha. She could only mumble out, "Yes, father!"

"What grave mistake were you about to commit? It would have been tragic!"

"I don't catch on, father?"

"What's wrong about that, my lord?" asked my mother, looking exceedingly bewildered.

My father then said, "All of you know well that right now that Sati is bound by her own commitment. She has been atoning for her moral failure. She must carry out all of it all alone. Don't give her any help. She can't violate the sanctity of her own ethical obligation. And, here, inadvertently, you have been trying to make her go on the wrong path! It's good that I've stopped you at the right moment!"

"Father!"

"Yes, Aditi?"

"All of us here now want to make a request to you."

"That's fine! What do you want to tell me?"

"How can Sati take on all that hardship?"

On that Prajapati Daksha said, "I just don't pay any attention to that issue. For me only the rules matter." He paused and observed our faces. "The entire world appreciates Prajapati Daksha's awareness of and love for justice. Only because of that, the people look up to me!" he added with a hint of pride in his voice.

"Don't the human feelings have any place in life, dear father?"

"Yes, they have! Why not?"

"Then why only Sati has been asked to go through such severe penance?"

Prjapati laughed. Then, looking at us, he said, "I don't love Sati less than anyone else. But ..."

Cutting in, my mother said, "But, what, my lord?"

"Prasuti!"

"Yes, my lord!"

Fixing his gaze on my mother's face, he said, his tone even and extremely neutral, "I'm not an unfeeling and cruel father!"

"When did I say that, my dear Lord?"

"Maybe, it's something there in your unconscious mind and, it's something that you aren't even aware of!"

"No! It isn't there at all!" My mother said and paused, musing over something. After a long silence, she whispered, "I can't bear Sati going through all that."

"Prasuti, I want to tell you something."

"Yes – my Lord!"

"You have full right that you should think about the well-being of your children. He kept quiet for a few moments and, then, he said, "But, all the same, you can't overlook the issue that's related to your husband's dignity."

"Your dignity is the first thing in my consideration, my Lord," said my mother in a meek tone.

Eyes closed, I had been listening to all that. Then opening my eyes, I mumbled in a low tone, "Father!"

"Yes, my dear", he said, concerned and eager.

"Even, I want to tell you something."

"Tell it. I'll listen to what you say with full attention!" he said, his voice full of intense emotion. He paused and brooded over something and, then, in an even tone, he let on, "Even I want to share something with you. I want to know your mind on a certain issue."

"Your words are a command for me, I said rather sentimentally.

His face beamed. His tone was full of love when he told me, "Daughter, tell me frankly if you have any doubts about my love for you!"

I was overcome by tender emotions in those moments. Holding his hands into mine, I said, "No! Not at all! Even an iota of doubt about it, would be a sin on my part. Father, your daughter is proud of your consideration. SheI love you have the greatest respect for you. I'm thankful for your thinking about me."

He was extremely delighted with my confession. He could not utter a single word for a long time. His voice almost choked up when he began saying, "My dear daughter, I'm extremely proud of you. In my eyes, you're a rare person. What has appealed to me greatly is the fact that you have been atoning for your failure so bravely. I appreciate your determination and, also the way that you have been carrying out my command. You make it look so spontaneous! I know that at the end of the day, you'll pass through this trial with flying colors."

My father's words and appreciation had revived my moribund spirit. I had understood that he had full faith in my ability. Not only that much, perhaps, secretly, he wished for my success too.

Overwhelmed with hitherto unfelt emotion, I touched his hands and said, "Father, I want to tell you something else too."

"Please do tell that to me, my beloved daughter! You've all authority over me."

I said, "Your commitment to rules and regulations and your awareness of dharma inspires me a lot. Motivates me so much so that I want to take after you too."

His face glowed. He mused over something before he said, "My darling daughter, I too want to tell you something." He stopped and gently passed his hand over my head. It delighted me. Then, looking at me, he began again, "Abiding by the rules of the state and the duties of a king, is of paramount importance. It contributes vastly towards the growth and betterment of any societycommunity. Today, in the capacity of a king and as a caretaker and protector of the people – those whom I govern and look after – I can say with absolute honesty that rules and regulations concerning the state and king's commitment to them and his people can't be overlooked and compromised with. Any laxity in the matter would bring about a sharp decline in the society and the people."

I remembered even the moment when the parijat flowers had slipped off from my hands and had spread all over the floor. In fact, I had staggered and could not keep my balance. I had begun picking them up.

"Your vow will have its completion," sage Dadhichi had whispered into my ears.

Grandfather Brahma could never much appreciate my father's vain pride. He could never forget how Shiva had cut off his fifth face and trampled over his pride. Now he was very worried about his own son, Daksha's pride. My father, Prajapati Daksha, had begun considering himself to be the director and preserver of the whole universe.

But, who can go against the force and law of destiny. My, father had compiled the Daksha Samhita – a book of rules and regulations. My father thought that more could go against the rules prescribed in his look. But what he was totally unaware of was that my Lord – Shiva – was beyond all those prescriptive codes. Also that he was the creator of yoga and, the lifestyle presented by him for others, was the best and the most original and creative in the world. The practitioner of this yoga system was given absolute freedom. An entirely new system of lifestyle was at the roots of devotion and commitment to Shiva. How could he be confined into the bounds of Daksha Samhita? And, he was the one who I had given my heart away to. That greatest yogi and, the one who was above all human desires and aspirations was now my absolute passion. I belonged to him and he, to me. His eternal company was now my only passion and longing in life. Destiny had been playing its own part. Maybe, I was just born for bringing that greatest yogi and detached soul-Shiva into the fold of a family men for the destruction of the forces of darkness in the world and for the preservation and betterment of mankind.

I needed rest. I was totally exhausted. I knew that Daksha Samhita could not have any effect upon Shiva. What was the truth after all? In fact, Shiva is the ultimate Director of the entire universe. There were only a few enlightened people who could perceive the aughar expression of Shiva's personality. My life's mission had become transparent before me. That was a metamorphosis of Shiva into a willing house holder.

Very tired, I had been lying on my bed. I had no awareness when I had fallen asleep. I had a dream. I had reached some exotic land. I loitered about that terra incognita. It was a beautiful place. Its verdure had a cooling effect upon my taut nerves. A cool breeze ruffled my hair and refreshed me. On every hand there were colorful flowers and other plants. A crystalline stream flowed through the place. Its murmuring gentle sound was musical. Soothed by it, I was softened to the core. Whatever had been happening within me in those moments had a numinous quality. I felt then as if all those things had been happening in my life in reality. My very being was softened. All dryness within me had been replaced by a feeling of vibrant joy. Those were the moments of ineffable ecstasy. I was certain that it was not any kind of hallucination. Then, suddenly, it became clear to me. My Lord was in the pose of yoga meditation. The snow had begun falling. It seemed as if Shiva had now rubbed all over his body the ashes of snow. His expansive and divine form was enhancing the fairness of that snow. I was now completely lost in the observation of phenomenon and had been totally oblivious of any other thing around me in those magical moments. It felt as if I was on a trance.

The moments passed.

"Sati!" someone gently called out.

"Who is there?"

"It's meI'm here! Look around!"

"You!"

"Yes-only I'm here! Why do you at all look so astonished?" he said with a smile.

Gazing at Shiva, I uttered, "How's it possible!"

"Nothing is impossible in this universe, Sati."

"I can't make out anything of it. It has boggled my mind. What has all been happening to me here?"

I blurted out in utter confusion, "I said, casting a sharp and questioning glance at him.

His intense love for me flashed in his eyes. Brooding over something for a few moments, he asked me," Don't you like this ambience?"

My response to his question was impulsive. "I've fallen in love with it. It seems to have captured my very fancy, my very heart." A silence ensued. I looked at him. His eyes were calm and impenetrable. "I don't feel like going away from here, I want to stay back here forever. Oh – how beautiful is the place! It takes away your ennui and torpor and gives you a deep insight into man's life.

With a smile, then my Lord said, "How practical you're, Sati! You offer a complete contrast to me."

"How?"

"I'm dull and unromantic".

"This isn't the truth," I said.

"Then what's the truth?"

"You're a highly romantic person. I'm very sure of it."

He laughed. I looked at him. he explained, "You'll be frustrated here!"

"It won't be so," I said emphatically.

"What gave you that impression?"

"I just felt like that," he said and began looking at me admiringly. "But what makes you so sure about it?" he asked, curious.

"I know my mind!"

"What gives you this tremendous strength and stability?"

"You risk a surmise."

"You won't be able to live at this place."

"Why can't I live here?"

Casting a glance at me, he explained, "Living here is a tough thingNo entertainment no luxuries. I wonder if a princess can adapt herself to the demands of this jejune place."

"I wonder at your innocence," I told him laughing.

"Why do you say that?" he asked.

I explained, "Don't you know that love is the greatest passion on earth? It's the all-consuming power in my view." I paused to search for more effective words. He just looked on. "For love only, even a princess can give up all luxuries and creature comforts," I added.

"Okay – let's dance now, Sati!" he proposed getting up from his place.

"How can I dance with you?"

"Why can't you?"

"Your dance is known all over the universe!" I said.

"So what?"

"I'm no match to you."

He laughed. "You aren't an ordinary dancer either. Even you've quite a reputation," he said to me.

"I think you've got wrong information about it."

He then told somewhat sarcastically, "You're right, Sati. Any surmise isn't a good thing. It's very difficult too. Nor is it very desirable either." He stopped for a few moments. Looking at him intently, I tried to guess his thoughts. I was totally confused and did not know how to get over that moment of incertitude. Then, he said, his tone eager and expectant, "However, it can only be decided after the dance. Step out of this state of uncertainty and, come along and dance with me."

He stretched out his hand. He seemed very happy in those moments. He had a strange and irresistible charisma about him. Everythingthe entire Creation seems to have been contained in those large eyes. His large, black matted locks of hair were very impressive. His fair complexion and expansive forehead and the crescent moon over there just enhanced his attraction. The snake around his neck and trisul and damru and the necklace of rudraksha beads reflected before others his divinity. In those moments, I longed for registering and enclosing his that image into my memory forever. I knew that everyone could not understand all that. But I was sure that I knew perfectly who he was. Maybe, I had secretly taken a vow that I would bring that Yogi Shiva into the fold of a family. The whole Creation is imperfect and meaningless without a togetherness of Shiva and Shakti.

"Okay – let's dance together", I said, holding his extended hand.

While dancing with him, I had lost awareness of time and space. I kept matching my footsteps with his. Our gestures and facial expressions matched too. Those were the moments of perfect harmony. Natraj Shivameaning Shiva the King of all dancers, was the most accomplished entity too. The sound of our dancing feet were resounding through the whole universe.

All night long, we danced together. A strange silence had set in too. It seemed to have spread all over the place. Shiva's very touch had thrilled me. I felt a strange and inexpressible sensation covering through my yielding body. It had a great divinity about it. It was an expansive momentpresence of love. It, undoubtedly, contained the will-being of the entire Universe.

It was something alive. It had all excitement. My entire being fluttered. I was flabbergasted. Just, in the beginning, all of it seemed to have been covered in a mist. But now, everything has become transparent. That vague image had now stepped out from that confusing state. The half of that figure was male and the other half was that of a female.

It confused me somewhat initially. But soon, I could make out that it was the Ardhanariswara –

the half man and the half woman- from of Shiva. The truth is that this is a universal phenomenon. In every man, there is a female, and vice versa. It confirms that eternal unity of Shiva and Shakti. It was a divinity in essence.

The morning approached. I had come out of that state of oblivion. After opening my eyes, I felt whatever I had experienced in my trance, was not at all real. Even then, I was inwardly convinced that I had danced all the night long with my dear Shiva. I had then felt as if the entire Creation was filled with the presence of Shiva.

Startled, I had sat up. I felt as if I could not free myself from the presence of my loved one. It felt as if he existed in the very core of my being. Perhaps, we were inseparable! I brooded over that. I thought over the whole thing intensely. I wondered if I was not working against and, inadvertently insulting my father by not separating myself totally from Shiva in thoughts and deeds. Otherwise, why had I been constantly dreaming of Shiva?

❑

The sky was overcast. There was a possibility of rains. I had set out for the collection of lotus flowers, I did not ask anyone to accompany me. Just then, it had begun raining cats and dogs. There was terrible thunder and flash of lightning in the sky occasionally. I wondered if, the others had set out in search of me too after realizing that I was not present in the palace.

I had reached the mountain where my dear Shiva would do meditation. I was lost in my own thoughts. All of a sudden, the sound of damru floated into my ears.

My eyes swimming in tears, in a weeping tone, I said, "Why have you been acting so strangely? Why have you been doing all these things to me? Have I offended you in any way to deserve all these things? Why can't I get rid of your presence from my life? Why can't I think about others? Don't you understand how you have been controlling my very life?"

Notwithstanding all that, I kept moving on. I was more determined now. Then, suddenly, I came upon some people strangers.

"What have you been doing here, princess?" one of them asked me respectfully?

Not a little shocked, I asked him, "I don't know you? Who are you?"

On that, the man spoke out, "Respected princess, I'm the same sculptor who had given you that Shiva-ling."

Very amazed, I asked him, "But, why have you been loitering about with your families here? Are you on some journey?"

The man then told me, "Princess, Prajapati Daksha has banished us from his kingdom! Now, we have all been looking for a new place where we can settle down!"

"Why has he expelled you?" The man said,"

"In his eyes, I'm an offender."

"Why so?"

"It's because I'd given you the Shiva-ling! Do you remember that, princess? It made him angry and, he has given us punishment!"

I was very confused. I did not know how to console him. At last, I could only utter in a very painful tone, "Please forgive me! Because of me you been are going through this hardship!"

In an extremely polite voice, the sculptor then spoke out, “Respected princess, I request you not to hold yourself responsible for our plight in any way!”

“Why shouldn’t I? After all, you have all been suffering only because of my action!” I said emphatically.

Overcome by emotions, that man said, “Don’t take it to your heart, princess!” He paused and fixed his gaze upon me. After a brief silence, he began again, “I’m not a learned person; but I know it well that each of has his own fate in this corporeal world. None can escape it!” He paused for a few seconds. I observed him. His face was calm and, he did not look disturbed. “Look after you!” he said in clear, even tone.

“I wish you the same!” I said to him.

“Where are you heading for, princess?” he asked me.

“I have been looking for the lotus flowers,” I told him.

His face beamed. He said, “Now don’t worry about anything, princess! There is a place where you can get infinite number of flowers from.”

“Where is it? Tell me the way”, I said eagerly.

His face became serious. “But!” he stopped in the middle.

“But…what? Tell me frankly,” I said.

"It's a very difficult place to reach. I wonder, how you'll reach there, he said, filled with doubts.

"Don't worry about the difficulties," I told him.

"Should we give you company?" he asked.

"No!"

"I worry about you!"

"I have to do it all alone! Thanks!"

On my insistence, he told me about the place. I thanked him and moved on. The sculptor was right. The place was far away and full of hazards.

While I was heading for the place to get the flowers, many thoughts came floating into my mind. I kept brooding over many incidents of the past. Many things that had happened in my life, I never wanted them to have happen. I wondered when I brooded over my father's hostility towards Shiva. Despite my best efforts, I could not think of any specific reason for it. The very name of Shiva angered my father.

While composing Daksha Samhita, my father had only prescribed the worship of Lord Vishnu. The name of Shiva had been deliberately counted out. I recalled the conversation between the great sage Narad and my father. Although they had the same genesis, they were exactly opposite to each other in every way.

"Are you, in any way, afraid of Shiva?" asked Narad.

"Why do you ask that?"

"Just tell me", Narad said.

"No! Not at all! Great Prajapati Daksha isn't afraid of anything!" He stopped. "But what do you want to point out?"

Narad said, "Then why haven't you made any reference to Shiva Puja in your book?"

My father then said, "I must clear up all your doubts. In my kingdom, there isn't any place for Shiva. If you wish, you can just go and tell him all that I've told you about him. He paused for some time, then, with a broad smile said, "You're quite an expert in flaring up an enmity".

Narad had burst out into laughter.

When he was going away, I had come across him.

"Where are you coming from, Sati?"

"My father has asked me to write the name of Lord Vishnu on a hundred thousand lotus flowers. I'd gone out, searching for them," I said.

"You have been asked to go through such harsh penance! Certainly, it must have been some big offence from your side!" he told me. I just kept quiet and began looking at him. he said again, "I bow before you and give my blessings from the very depths of my heart."

"I don't deserve this reverence, dear Sir. I'm confused. I don't understand much of your statement", I said, looking at him fixedly.

A smile came across him face. He said to me, "I have been told how you called Shiva here when the idol of Lord Vishnu was being set up here!"

"Only for that mistake...offence I have been atoning for now, sir," I told in a sad voice. He looked at me in a strange and amused way. "I shouldn't have violated the code and generosity of my father!" I added with a whisper.

He smiled and then said, "Eternally, he is dressed up as a Yogi. His simplicity and innocence are legendary. I wonder how a princess can overlook it and fall in love with him! Give up all comports and luxuries and violate all rules and codes of life!"

"Don't use such words against him, sir," I said, my voice slightly indignant.

He laughed at my reaction. His face beamed with happiness. He then told me, "Whatever you say Sati, I feel, in any dress, Shiva stands out in any gathering! The Lord is a real charmer!"

His words had pleased me immensely. In those moments I felt that he knew everything about us I mean whatever had been going on between Shiva and me. However, I thought that the topic was to be changed and, any continuation of that might create further complication. So, bowing before him, I sought his permission to go away from there.

In those moments, my sole mission was to make my father happy. I wanted to convince him that his daughter was very obedient and had all respect towards her father. And, for the cause of her father's honor, she could go to any extent. My father had asked me not to eat anything and, even drink water. I had lost my appetite and, did not even have an urge for drinking water. I had just been putting up with all those hardships only because I wanted my father to get over his feeling of hurt. I must also tell here how sage Narad had mentioned casually during the talks between us that my last and final destination was only Shiva. As far as I'm concerned, even I was fully convinced of it. Inwardly, I knew that Sati was born to be with her dear one only. And, he was none other than Shiva himself.

While writing the name of Lord Vishnu, a moment came when I had passed out for some time. I was terribly exhausted. Even in my that swoon, I was sensible of his cosmic form: his dancing that formidable trisul, his damru's entrancing sound that would echo through the entire cosmos and, above all these, his that handsome and prepossessing figure wrapped in a deer skin. I could feel then all that happening to me. All the night long, my Lord had danced with me. His cool and soothing touch had gone deep into my very being. It had a quality of lastingness. Everything was transparent now. He was willing to share his space with me.

I did not share all that with anyone. That was my private self and, in any case, was not to be shared with others. But I could feel that my Aditi Didi was not very sure about my intention. Overcome by all sorts of doubts, she kept observing my actions and reactions minutely. But I knew whatever I had experienced in that state of mine was not just a vaporous dream. It was something concrete and had taken place in my life in actuality. And, the truth is, I don't have any doubts about it that it was part of my Lord's leela. It was the most difficult thing to find out to know his real intention.

To get all those lotus flowers was a very difficult task. My limbs had begun bleeding. I was going through all those hardships willingly. However, it had depressed all others very much. It was a self-imposed thing on my part. All the time it was a kind of self-flagellation. Even my father felt that he had taken a wrong decision. I was very pained when I came to know that he too was not taking any food because of me.

The task had been completed. I opened the door and came out. I felt all in, and my voice had because very low on account of weakness and, yet, my face beamed. I had finished everything on time. While completing the task, I was totally oblivious of my physical needs. During the period, I did not eat anything, nor was I even aware of the sores and blisters in my hands. I was just conscious of one thing: that I had to write the name of Lord Vishnu on those lotus flowers.

On seeing that glow on my face, all could make out that I had completed the task successfully.

"Let me embrace you, my dear daughter'" my mother said to me with the utmost warmth.

Tears filled my eyes. Voice changed with overpowering emotions, I said, "Mother, you're the very plinth of your daughter!"

All my sisters were happy too. They embraced me one by one.

My father had reached there too. It was clear to him that I had completed the task. He said, his voice full of warmth, "I'm very proud of you, my dearest daughter! You've restored my lost respect today. I'm grateful to you. Thanks!" He stopped briefly and cast a loving glance at me. In those moments he was not the great Prajapati. He was just a doting father. "Daughter you're my very pride, my dignity and my grace," he added.

"Dear father, at least, keep some of your love safe for us too," said Khyati Didi jokingly.

"Don't be jealous of your younger sister, Khyati. This isn't a good thing," retorted father in the same spirit.

A soft redolence of warm love had spread over the place. In those moments I could realize how beautiful a thing was the harmony and goodwill among the members of a family! Even Prajapati Daksha had lost control over himself then. He was then only a doting father and nothing more. Prasuti, my mother, was looking at that great, emotional family drama fondly. Her eyes were sparkling with pride. How beautiful was that scene! The whole room was filled with the flowers with the name of the Lord written on them. Overcome by emotions, his eyes shone with the utmost brightness. Even two of my saptarshi brothers-in-law had reached there.

Looking at all of them, my father said, "My daughter, Sati, is the best among all my other daughters. I don't have even an iota of doubt in declaring that she is my true heir! I, her father, am immensely proud of her at this moment!"

Afterwards, bending down, he had picked up one flower. Immediately his face lost its color. Intense anger seemed to have replaced that kind look that was there on his countenance a few moments ago. No longer was his face proud of me. He fumed and hissed. His eyes coruscated. Stunned, we kept looking at him. When my mother tried to talk to him, he stopped her brusquely. Before we could guess anything, he walked away from there.

A painful silence ensued for a few moments. All of us were filled with doubts and ill-omen about the future. Then, Khyati Didi picked up a flower.

"What have you done here, Sati," she cried out in consternation.

The flower had slipped out from her hand. Then, I picked that up. A shudder ran down my body. I now knew the reason of my father's anger. On all those flowers was written the name of Shiva. I thought over that and, apparently, I could not make out how that had happened at all. Tears ran down my eyes.

I went to my father and said, "Father, I'm your daughter and loyal to you to the core. I'm not mean as to go against your wishes and violate your orders." When I paused to take a breath, he had begun looking at me, his face was impassive. "Father, I cannot commit the grave sin of telling a lie before great Prajapati Daksha. Believe me, I had only written the name of Lord Vishnu on those flowers. I don't know how it changed into Shiva.

My father did not speak out anything and remained calm too. The silence around us was rather painful.

After some time, gently he passed his hand over my bent head and, said in his sweetest voice, "Now, get up, Sati! This isn't your fault at all. The truth is that I myself am to blame for it. I failed in assessing the situation!" He then paused and instructed the maids, "Throw away those flowers and get some food for Sati!"

And, when he put the first morsel into my mouth, I was overpowered by his warmth and my emotions.

"Father!"

"Yes, Sati!" He stopped for a few moments. I looked at him. His eyes were full of expansive love.

"Don't keep any load over your mind now, Sati. The bad phase is over," he added, his tone moist with sentiments.

"I was terribly frightened!" I uttered, shuddering.

On that he said, "I love you immensely, Sati. Even in my wildest dream, I can't visualize your being in the company of that undisciplined, slovenly aughad Shiva!" I did not utter a single word in opposition. However, I was deeply hurt by his utterance. He went on, "Now, put aside everything. The spring season festivities are about to begin. I hand over the charge of the entire celebration to you. Its splendor and success will confirm your talent before others. I trust your abilities!

"Thank you, father! I love you!" I uttered gratefully.

Then, turning to mother, Prajapati said, "I find this palace transformed into a big desert in absence of Sati, Prasuti."

"Don't be exceedingly emotional", said my mother humorously.

"Why shouldn't I, Prasuti?"

It's not a very healthy thing. It might even hurt a person!"

"Sati can never hurt me", said my father.

"I was just joking, great Prajapati". Then, father said, "The groom I wish for her should be the one who would accept to live with us here, in our palace."

Laughing softly, then said my mother, "How could you utter that thing, my husband?"

"What's wrong about that, Prasuti?"

"Don't forget our tradition!"

You don't overlook the emotional aspect," said my father rather loudly".

On that my mother said, "My husband, every daughter has to go away from her father's house one day. O, great Prajapati, you too can't look down upon the tradition. You'll have to rise above this, moha! It doesn't become you at all."

Father's voice was very serious when he said, "You're right. Thanks! Even then I want to tell you something." When he paused, my mother looked at him and tried to guess what was going on in his mind. He began again, "Shiva Bhakt like Dadhichi has left a left a deep impression on the mind of Sati. It'll be a tough task to wipe out all that from her mind. I'll put in my intense efforts for that. I wouldn't let Shiva be a winner. I have to fulfill the duties of a father. I've handed over the charge of the spring season festivities to Sati. I'll put in all my efforts in turning her attention away from Shiva." He stopped briefly, groping for more effective words. My mother could guess my father's fears and frustration. Then, breaking that long, heavy silence, my father began again, "Prasuti, Shiva can't take my daughter away from me. I'll frustrate all his plans against me."

On hearing my father's words, my mother tried to console him, "Dear husband, don't let these events upset you at all. I'm Sati's mother. I know her character very well. She is an ideal daughter. She'll never let her parents feel small before others for her own comforts and selfish ends. She'll never do anything to hurt their dignity. I assure you fully on her behalf."

Our maids had gone out to dispose off those flowers.

"Shiva has been written on all these", observed one of them.

"How does it matter Chandrika?"

Chandrika said, "You aren't very perceptive, Malya!"

"How do you perceive it Chandrika?"

"This apparent indifference may make Shiva angry," said Chandrika.

Satya cut in, "No-! It can never be so!"

"Why can't it be so, Satya?" asked all of them in unison.

Looking at them, Satya said, "Shiva is very kind and magnanimous. We're just maids. Our job is to act on the orders of our master. In no case can we ignore the orders of our master, Prajapati Daksha." After keeping quiet for some time, she added, "Don't forget how harsh a punishment Prajapati had imposed upon his own daughter. What status do we hold in this matter? Be a realist. Never ever forget that we're just maids! That's our identity!"

"You have been telling the truth, Satya! We shouldn't indulge in any complexity," said Malya in a low tone".

They were about to discard those flowers when someone reached there.

"What are you doing of these flowers?"

"We've been throwing these away on behest of our master, Prajapati Daksha.

"How rare and beautiful these flowers are!" cried out that man emotionally. Then, after a brief pause, he said, "Could you give these flowers to me?"

"What would you do of these flowers, stranger?" asked Malya casually.

"These aren't of any use. That's why we have been asked to do away with them! Said Chandrika to him.

"These flowers won't be of any use to anyone," pointed out Satya.

"It doesn't matter at all. I find them priceless," he said with the utmost reverence.

"How?" all of them asked together.

"Shiva's name has been written on them!"

"Are you a devotee of Shiva?" asked Malya.

"Yes- I am."

"Even then we can't hand over these flowers to you at our own will," said Chandrika.

"That's fine! You go and get the permission of princess Sati," said the stranger.

Malaya went in and came back in a few minutes with the permission of Sati.

"That's fine. We've got the permission, but now the princess herself is coming over here. You've got to wait for a few minutes."

When Sati had reached there that stranger tried to touch her feet.

"Oh- what's this? Why have you been trying to touch my feet? You're very senior to me, I said.

The stranger spoke out, "Mother, by touching your feet, I feel blessed in every way!" He cast a pleading glance at me then, he asked, "Could I take these flowers with me?"

My brother-in-law had recognized Nandi even in his that makeup. Even my father had reached that place as he had some work with me. He flew off the handle. He felt as if Shiva had sent Nandi there to get all those flowers. Shiva had not paid any heed to Prajapati's warning. Nandi's presence there was the most unwanted thing for my father.

While collecting all those flowers, Nandi kept on muttering, "Mother, I have been really blessed todayMy life has been elevated to a higher point."

He left the place with all those flowers. Once more sadness had set in our place. My father was now even not listening to my mother. I could not determine why my father was so angry then. But I could know it when sage Kashyap explained the real thing to me.

Shiva is known as a magnanimous giver. Right from my very childhood I was attracted towards him. At the time I would see my father offering water to Lord Vishnu. He would collect the water into a conch and offer it to his Lord. When I wanted to offer water in the name of Shiva in the same way, I was told the story of the demon Sankhchud and how the demon had secured the boon of immortality from Brahmadeva and Lord Vishnu and how he was burnt down and reduced to ashes by the searing glance of Shiva's third eyes. His wife, Tulsi, was very devoted and pure person. The conch was made out from the bones of Sankhchud. So, the water is offered to Lord Vishnu through a conch but not to ShivaThere are countless such stories in circulation in our country.

I was now fully determined to win Shiva's love in any way. It was now my sole purposemission in life to win Shiva in his original form for me. Nandi prayed to Shiva to accept me as his wife. But Shiva was lost in his profound meditation once more. Dejected greatly, Nandi had floated all those flowers into the river.

❑

My father tried very hard to distract my attention from Shiva. He called in all the five elements: fire, water, wind, the sky and the earth to help him. He put a grain of rice before him and, even after using their all might they could not even budge it a little bit. In fact, father was trying to display his own might before me. He even wanted to suggest to me that by attracting me towards him, the sole intention of Shiva was to cause pain to my father and make him feel small.

His words had begun having their effect upon me too. I had now decided that I would not let myself be a tool of Shiva. I would not at all let him use me as an instrument for causing suffering to my dear ones.

Everything was going on well. Perhaps, deliberately Nandi had left one flower behind him at that place. I had picked up that flower. That one flower had reached up to Shiva and touched his feet. At that very moment. I knew about my ultimate destination.

Prajapati had called in a big meeting at his place. Shiva had not participated in it. It was meant to find out about the functioning of the entire world. But it had a secret agenda too. Shiva had cut off, the one head of Brahmadeva, the father of Prajapati. Besides that, I had also fallen in love with Shiva. My father was thinking of eliminating the name of Shiva forever from the list of divinities. Therefore, he has called in this meeting at his place.

Chandrama had reached there with Rohini and Revati Didi. I had to welcome all three of them. Holding the hand of Rohini Didi, Chandrama had moved forward. Revati Didi was left slightly behind. And, when I asked her to move forward then, hesitantly, moving up, she stood by the side of her spouse.

"Didi are you happy with your husband?"

I asked her rather bluntly when I found her alone after some time.

Flashing a made-up smile, she said, "What sort of question is this, Sati? Every woman is happy with her life partner."

I told her, my voice sharp, "I feel you have been telling a lie!"

Turning her back on me, she uttered, "Sati, don't put up to me any more questions."

"What's that? Don't I have any right over you?"

"Yes – you have."

"Then?"

"Many questions cannot be answered", she almost said rather incoherently.

Before I could put up further questions, she burst into tears. Perhaps, she now wanted to reduce the burden of sole.

"Tell me the truth Didi," I insisted.

"You're incorrigible!" she said as if surrendering before me.

"You must tell everything to me now," I said in a peremptory voice.

Her voice was calm and stable when she said, "The social system is very cruel. It's totally apathetic towards the feelings of women. Ruthlessly it crushes down the heart of a woman. Her role has been reduced to looking after his male. Also she must fulfill without any complaint all his needs." Her eyes shone and her voice became louder. She said, "This is a meaningless thought, an empty one. It's based on the exploitation of women. It aims at putting shackles around her feet."

"What a wonderful thinker you are, didi," I said appreciatively.

She went on, her voice full of confidence now, "In our society almost no attention is paid to the desire and dignity of a female. She is just an object of lust, to be enjoyed at will."

"Didi, be candid about your own relationship with your husband." She looked at me sharply. "You can trust me," I said to assure her. "Whatever, you share with me, remains between us only," I added in a calm voice.

On my assurance, she felt relaxed. After a brief silence she said, "Men are fickle-minded. Our society has bestowed all freedom upon a male. He can choose any one at his whim fancy. A relationship is his privilege."

Then, I said, my voice bitter and sharp, "Even women should have such freedom too!"

Revati Didi laughed and said, "You're a grown-up woman now, Sati! She kept quiet for some time. The, she told, "Chandra, your brother-in-law and my husband is a very fickle minded person!?"

"Does he insult you? I asked her. Resting her gaze on my face, she said, her voice exceedingly sad, "Insult is one thing and its painful undoubtedly; but apathy is the most tragic thing in the life of a woman. A woman can put up with her husband's temper and, at times, even enjoy it secretly; but she fades out, even ceases to be with the cold indifference of her life-partner." She paused. Perhaps, she was thinking about her own relationship with her husband. When she began speaking out again, she was the very image of suffering, "I don't know Sati, how long I can put up with all this! As far as my husand is concerned, in his life only Rohini exists. Don't think I'm jealous of my own sisterBut the only thing that I can tell you now is this that Rohini owns Chandra in every way."

Her inward suffering had perturbed me greatly. Holding her hands tenderly into mine, I tried to console her. But I knew that my efforts were in vain. Her bitterness was deep-seated. There was no cure for it. Her acceptance of her own fate and situation was a tragic reality.

The magnitude of the gathering at my father's place was vast. Some of the visitors were awed by the grandeur of my father's lifestyle. And, there were some others who were secretly jealous of his infinite resourcefulness and affluence. Even the spring season festival had begun. My sisters had presented before others their musical talents. When it was my turn then, all of them had begun looking at me curiously. I took up the veena and, after closing my eyes, began playing on it. Although I was playing on it, the notes produced seemed to have been issuing from the Shiva veena. In those precious moments, my entire being seemed to have been flooded by the very presence of Shiva. The professional dancers had been dancing to my tune. Madnika had understood that it was a tune of Shiva. I had begun singing. All present there seemed to have been drowned in the sweetness of the musical notes. My lips were quivering and, the big tear drops had begun streaming down my eyes. All around me, I was sensing Shiva's divine presence.

Suddenly, some other musical notes had begun floating into that song. It was the most charismatic moment in my life. I did not know when my feet had begun dancing on those notes of the veena. Shiva was playing the veena and, I was dancing around, totally forgetting everything, to that sweet, resounding notes of the veena. Time seemed to have lost its movement. I was intoxicated by those melodic notes of his music. Both, Shiva and I had begun looking at each other fondly. Those were the great moments. Instinctively, I had perceived then that Shiva was there with me. The message was clear to me.

Aditi didi and Khyati didi were very angry with me.

"You had gone out to get water, Sati! Where is your vessel?" had asked Khyati didi.

I just looked at her. I was still under the spell of that music. Those musical notes lingered on. I had been the winner in that competition.

I came back to my own self when Aditi didi shouted, "You have forgotten all etiquettes now!"

"Sorry, didi! Be generous! I'm helpless against the onslaught of love!"

Khyati didi burst out, "You're a fool, Sati!"

"How? I need a convincing explanation!"

Then, casting a searing glance at me, she said, "That Shiva is inciting you against your own father.

I already see an undisciplined rebel in you. For quite some time now, you have been acting against all decency. Now, you look down openly upon any kind of courtesy." She paused. Her lips fluttered with anger. I observed that she was groping for words that would hurt me with greater effectiveness. At the end, she said venomously, "That Shiva can never succeed against our great father!"

I laughed. She tried to impale me with her gaze. I mumbled, "You're being driven on by malice and prejudice. That's the reason why your mind isn't in control over your reactions Right now, your assessment is unacceptable, didi. I reject it outright."

Losing control over her completely, she shouted," You're a victim of the worst obsession, Sati! You're a lost person. I feel for you only because you're my dear sister or else, I'd have turned my back on you long back. I love you and I want to redeem you for sure!"

Lost in my own thoughts, I just mumbled, "I had lost my awareness in the sweetness of these notes didi! Drawn into their vast expanse, I had been transported into some other world!" I stopped for some time and then went on, "Only Shiva could have enlivened those dormant notes. And he did so. He had brought them to life.

Both, Aditi didi and Khyati didi kept quiet.

I had gone out with Madanika one day. She was very close to my mother. But she loved me a lot.

She was very proud of my being the winner of the competition.

While we were walking, she said to me all of a sudden, "Sati, I'm a court dancer." I looked at her questioningly. "So, my foremost loyalty is towards love. I believe that love is powerful enough to transform everything.

"Madnika!"

"Yes, Sati!"

"You're a lovable person," I said and looked at her appreciatively.

"Thanks, Sati!" she said gently.

"Further..."

"Yes, Sati!"

"You're very understanding too!"

"Thanks again, Sati!" After pausing briefly, she went on," The truth is, love doesn't have any cult or religion. It doesn't accept any taboos and binding either. You can't resist it oppose it. It's the biggest force. None can have control over it at one's whim or will. It's an invincible passion in all living beings."

When she stopped, I said, "Madnika, you've explained the thing in a brilliant manner." Her face glowed with happiness at my appreciation of her observation. Seeing that, so kingly, I added, "You seem to have been a great lover yourself, Madnika. That's my impression about you!"

She looked sharply at me. I knew that she was very delighted by my statement. She said, "Sati, what's your view about love?"

I cast an intense gaze at her. When our eyes met, she flashed a charming smile at me. When, I began speaking, my voice was full of warmth, "Madnika" I said, "love is the sweetest and succulent attribute. It is capable of giving a vast, illimitable expanse to a person. A lover is never afraid of anything. The moment one steps on the boat of love, he isn't afraid of getting drowned anymore into the choppy waves of the dark and angry water.

"The reason is very clear. He is already drowned in the ocean of love."

Both of us laughed freely. Then, holding the hand of each other, we walked on.

Then, Madnika and I had been separated. It seemed to me then as if some unknown power was drawing me towards it. Although I was a little apprehensive, I was convinced too as if some unknown being was at work for my safety.

I kept moving on. Suddenly, I was overtaken by a huge and violent cyclone. I felt as if I saw a terrible figure in that. His teeth were big and his nails big, black and sharp and threatening. Fear had gripped me then. I tried hard to get away from it. For some time, I was being told the stories about the demon Vrittasur. All of a sudden, I felt as if my own energy was getting reduced. The very thought of Vrittasur had given me gooseflesh. Maybe, the demon was playing some kind of game with me. All confused, I began running here and there. I had lost the sense of directions. Making a violent circular movement, the demon had reached up to me. I felt that he wanted to abduct me. He was trying to suck me into its nucleus. I felt then whatever it was, I would not be able to save myself from that demon.

"Where are you Shiva? Save me from the demon!" I cried out in despair.

The moment I uttered those words, all that commotion around me stopped. The powerful, vibrant notes of the damru echoed all around me. Shiva's all powerful trisul loomed up before me and began moving all around me. It was effectively driving back that cyclone from me. That cyclone could not touch my body. Instinctively, I knew that I had been saved.

It changed. My master was near me. I could feel his assuring presence all around me. I felt the sweet touch of his hand. First, he stood before me in the form of a bright luminescence. He stood as a wall between Vrittasur and me. Holding my arm, Shiva had pulled me away. How sweet was that touch with its intoxicating effect! That demon knew now that he had lost the struggle. So to save his own life, he had fled away from there.

"What for have you been loitering around in this sequestered place in this violent weather?" Shiva asked me in a peremptory voice. After a brief silence, he asked again, "Aren't you afraid of all this?"

"No-! I'm not afraid of anything," I said, laughing softly.

"Why?"

"I'm fully aware of my security," I said with pride.

"Don't be under any illusion, Sati!"

On that, I said, my tone having a hint of sarcasm, "I'm not; but you seem to be under one!"

"I'm under some illusion! Did you say that?"

"Yes, I did say that."

"How do you vindicate your statement?"

"When the time comes, it'll be all justified!"

"I think you don't have objectivity!"

"You're free to interpret it in your own way," I said laconically.

"What do you want from me after all?"

"I don't have to state anything. You're the master of this whole creation. You're fully aware of what has been happening here."

"Sati!"

"Shiva!"

"Now – go back home. Your parents must be worrying about you!"

"Why do you try to shun my company?"

"What do mean by that? He asked.

"Do you love me?" I asked boldly.

"What gave you this idea?"

"First you have got to give answer to my question."

"You must know it, Sati," he said in a cold voice. "I'm an ascetic, indifferent to the worldly activities and pleasures. What would you get from me?"

"Love!"

"I don't know what love is!"

"Then why do come to save me wherever I'm in trouble. It doesn't become an ascetic?"

"I can't see you suffer Can't see you in any trouble either."

I laughed. "I know what you feel about me, Shiva," I said rather flirtatiously.

"Now, you must go away from here, Sati. This isn't a very safe region," he said, concerned.

His words suggested immense love. A sweet sensation coursed through my body. I knew well that his character was very simple. His words contained a hint for my future. Brooding over my encounter with him, had cleared up my doubts. I was now inundated with powerful emotions.

I had returned. On the way, I met Madnika. She was worried about me and, had been trying to locate my whereabouts. The moment she saw me, her face flushed with joy. Her face expressed how relaxed she was now.

"Where have you been to, Sati?"

"How terrible the weather was, Madnika!"

"Are you okay?"

"Yes – I am."

I kept quiet. I did not share my that experience with her. We had come back home. By now, I had understood that my life was absolutely meaningless without the company of Shiva.

My father, Prajapati Daksha, was a victim of a false conviction. It made him ignorant and proud. All those who knew him were afraid of his highhandedness. He considered Shiva his greatest enemy. My father always reacted violently on hearing any praise of Shiva from the mouth of my grandfather.

"Only Shiva had cut off your head, father?"

"What do you want to tell me, Daksha?"

"I don't understand your character! For nothing, you keep praising that kapali, aughad Shiva. His very lifestyle is disgusting. Maybe, you aren't aware of his true character!" said my father in a voice a full of disrespect.

"Daksha!"

"Yes! What do you want tell me?"

"Your words give me a terrible picture of a dark future It's destruction all around!"

"Don't worry about my future, father!"

"Why shouldn't I?"

"I think you fear my opposing Shiva, don't you?" He paused briefly. Then, he told, "Shiva can't do anything to me!" Shocked, the grandfather kept quiet.

After getting back, I had gone into my chamber. While changing my dress, I noticed on my arm the fingerprints of Shiva, I knew well now that he had given his approval for the alliance.

The entire Creation looked forward to the union of Shiva with me.

Shiva with bhasm all over his body was the most wonderful sight. Sitting on the skin of a tiger, gave Shiva a unique majesty. He would sit before a burning pyre and engage Nandi and Narad and other aghories in the most inscrutable discussions. He could brood over the most complex issues even there. There only could he do his profoundest meditation. The doubts he had were if a princess who had been brought up in the midst of all comforts and riches would be able to put up with all that.

I was reminded of the beauty contest. Everybody was busy discussing over Rohini didi and Revati didi. They were convinced that one of them could be the winner. Longingly Revati didi was looking at her husband Chandrama. But his gaze was only fixed on Rohini didi. But the moment I reached there they had begun looking at me. All present there then felt that only I would win the contest.

"Rohini, just look at Sati! She has grown into a real charmer! She must be married to someone soon," my said happily. Then dropping her voice into a whisper, she mumbled, "But, where do we get a match for her?"

On that I muttered inwardly, "Dear mother, I've already found out my spouse!"

My mother spoke up again, "My son-in-law should be equally handsome and prepossessing! Not only that, he should be perfect in carrying out his worldly obligations in a perfect manner."

I laughed inwardly. "Mother, your son-in-law is a perfect and supreme Yogi. He is indifferent to the world. He is handsome beyond words. But one needs a great perspicacity to see that charm.

On seeing the impression of fingers on my arms, Rohini didi took me to her chamber. She asked in a harsh voice, "Sati! What's this on your arm?"

I told her, "For saving me from Vrittasur, Shiva had reached there. The demon had almost swallowed me up." I stopped my eyes had moistened. I went on, "Shiva got up from his meditation and had reached there to save me. It was then that I saw a deep love for me in his eyes. It was a divine experience."

Rohini didi shook my shoulder as I was completely absorbed in my reminiscences. When I looked at her, she said, her voice sharp, "Have you ever thought over the consequences of it?"

"What's that?"

"It'll be a disastrous revelation for Prajapati Daksha."

I asked her, "Can anyone resist love?"

"One can," she said.

"I only love Shiva," I uttered in a low voice." No one else can replace him now!" I added.

"I don't know what has taken hold of you. I think it's one of those demons of the manipulative Shiva.

"Don't use that kind of language for the one who I love so much," I said, protesting. I began again, "There was once a time when you yourself used to tell that love was irresistible. What has happened to you now?"

"But, right now, I've been warning you against this infatuation of yours!"

"I can't go back now. I've covered a long distance," I said.

"Be sensible, Sati."

"It's impossible now. My entire consciousness is focused on Shiva now. He exists in every cell of my body He's now my very breath," I said in a firm voice.

"Okay-Sati! Now only Narayan will look after everything," said Rohini didi sadly, heaving a deep sigh.

... I had reached Kailash one day.

"Why have you come here, Sati?"

"I felt like meeting you!"

"Why?"

"Only, you have to look for the answer to this why?"

"Prajapati Daksha's daughter shouldn't have come over to this place without the permission of her father", he said. "I think it's wrong", he added to explain to me.

Without any hesitation, I said, "I can't help it now."

"Why?"

"You know it."

"I don't," he said.

"Should I then tell you the reason?"

"You must."

My voice firm and stable, I said, looking at him fixedly, "You've now complete command over my heart and mind. You can't deny the truth."

He said, "Love is a vast ocean, Sati. And I should tell you one thing here." He stopped and I looked at him yearningly. "I'm not without any tender feelings. I'm not a dull and unromantic person either. But, as far as you're concerned, I have nothing to give you. You had better go back to your own people. Those who love you.

I had come back with all the agony of separation in my heart. My dear one had rejected me. I now suffered from the pangs of unrequited love.

But my heart did not accept it. At my residence a marriage ceremony of Tulsi and Saligram was being performed. While I was listening intently to the story of Tulsi and Saligram I was seeing the image of my dear Shiva even in that Saligram. I wondered if both, Shiva and Vishnu, were only the pieces of stone. Vishnu in the form of Saligram and Shiva, in the form of Shivaling. However, Vishnu could step out of the stone and merge with the vibrant and living world. But Shiva only wants to remain a piece of stone. I had now made up my mind to bring him out from that stone form of his. He will have to come out from that inanimate state! I was doing the pooja of Saligram as if he were just Shivaling.

❑

Love is the greatest giver. It cannot be a beggar in any circumstances. For me Shiva was the supreme symbol of love. But, in contrast to that, my father considered the trivialities of life to be the foremost mission of a man. He even overlooked his own father, Brahmadeva, on several occasions. Once he had even become cross with his son-in-law Chandradeva because the latter had suggested to Prajapati to call in Shiva for my treatment. Once when my father had cursed Shiva, then my grandfather Brahmadeva had declared that none in the universe had the power of stopping the marriage of Sati with Shiva.

My mother, Prasuti, was devoted wholly to my father. She could not even dream of going against her husband even in her wildest dream. Often, she told me about the duties of an ideal daughter. The days had been passing quickly. All day and night long, I heard the resounding sound of the damru. Life had lost all charm for me. Without Shiva, it was not worth living. A big void seemed to have swallowed me. Each passing day only added to my ennui.

Once I had decided to go on dancing till Shiva reached there and joined me. While dancing around all over my chamber, I had become oblivious of all other things around. In my frenzied state of my mind, I felt as if my dear Shiva had come to dance with me. The dance that I had started with a slow motion, had reached soon a state of fury. There was something extremely exotic about that. It was a combination of divinity and physicality.

Holding me into his arms, Shiva was himself absorbed in that momentous dance. Exulted and elevated to the highest level of being, I felt as if our that motion was creating unfathomable void and, the entire universe was being sucked into that.

"Shiva!" I whispered.

"Yes-Sati?"

"What makes you so cruel?"

"I don't think it's the right observation," he refused to accept my statement.

"Yes-you are."

"This is just your fancy!"

"I know the true reason."

"Do you?"

"Yes."

"Tell me."

"You won't accept it."

He smiled. "I'll if it is logical."

"You have been faking indifference."

"How do you get that impression, Sati?"

"There is a reason for it."

"Is there one?"

"Yes."

"Tell it!"

"You just want to punish me because of my father!"

"That's a revelation, Sati! How?"

"My father had cursed you once!"

"I've already forgotten it."

"I want to say smoothing else."

"Yes – you can," he said, curious.

"You're a cold-blooded lover."

He curst into laughter. "I don't have any love in my life, Dakshayani!"

"Don't address me as Dakshayani!"

"What's there now?" he asked, surprised.

"I feel a greater identification with Sati!"

"Should I tell you a secret, Sati?"

"Secret? Yes, tell me."

"When I'm all alone in that endless silence of Kailash, I remember you fondly."

My face brightened up. "Then why don't you take me along with you there?" I asked.

"I can't go against the rules of the society."

"What rules have you been talking about?" I asked, slightly confused.

"The rules of marriage. Your father, Prajapati Daksha abhors my very presence. And, Sati, I can't take you away without his consent."

I was inwardly delighted with his awareness of the ethical values of life. "I thank you from the very depths of my heart," I said.

"What do you thank me for?"

"For teaching me the importance of morality in one's personal life," I uttered spontaneously in appreciation.

He changed the topic. "Do you still want to dance?"

"Why? Are you bored?"

"No! I'm enjoying myself happily."

"Then what?"

"This dance must have done you in!"

"I can go on dancing like this for eons." I paused. He looked at me. I said, "With you, I don't need any rest."

"Have you been telling the truth?"

"Veracity of my statement is unquestionable," I said with pride.

"Sati!"

"Shiva! My dear Lord!"

"Don't look at my love with any suspicion on your mind."

"How could you believe that I would ever doubt your intention? Your love is the purest one and, I know it well."

"Sati! I must tell you something else too."

"Tell me. I'm very eager and excited." With a smile on his face, he said, while looking at me intensely, "I wouldn't let you remain at your father's place for a long time. It's just a matter of time. Destiny is driving us on towards a union."

I laughed. Delighted to the core. "I'll wait for you."

How long the dance went on I could not know. No one else was aware of it either. A swoon had come over me before my father could reach there, Shiva had left the place. I had gone into a Yoganidra.

Khyati didi had given me the account of the sequence of events. A Rajvaidya had felt my pulse.

"This isn't some ordinary faint Prajapati. In fact, this isn't any kind of a swoon at all."

"When will she come to?" My mother had asked.

"Yoganidra is always unpredictable, Maharani." He stopped and looked at my mother. "I'm helpless at this point, he said."

"What's the care for it?" she asked.

"It depends on Sati's own will. No medicine will be effective in it."

"Why can't it be effective?" asked my mother.

The Vaidya then said, "This is finally related to man's microscopic consciousness. The truth is, it's beyond my science and skill."

Time passed. My mother was greatly concerned.

"I want to tell you something, mother," said Khyati didi.

"What do you want to tell me, Khayati?"

"You won't mind it!"

"No – I won't mind anything. You just tell me."

"Only, Shiva can bring her back to consciousness."

"How is it possible, Khyati?"

"Why isn't it possible?"

"Your father can never accept this proposal." "Why don't you persuade him, mother? Sati's life is what matters most now! Father's pride shouldn't a stumbling block on it," said Khyati didi in a resounding voice.

Prajapati Daksha had rejected the proposal. He told, "It won't be a right thing to call in that mountebank Shiva for curing Sati. I can't accept him at all as medical man – a physician."

...Even in that comatose state, I was, in a way conscious of the events happening around. I could hear everything. Then, I felt, as if someone was trying to nurse me back to health. Someone touched me tenderly. He had been whispering something into my ears too. Even in that Yoganidra I could make out that it was a touch from my dear Lord.

"Come back to your waking self, Sati," Shiva crooned into my ears.

"Have you come here, Shiva?"

"Come out of this Yoganidra, Sati," Shiva ordered me lovingly.

I came to. Shiva was standing before me. His eyes were glowing with immense love. It was all very transparent. No one else was around us then. Silently, for a long time, we had been looking at each other. Afterwards, Shiva had left the place.

Before parting, Shiva had said humorously "Sati, you're a very accomplished dancer."

With equal playfulness, I said to him, "But, you alone hold the title of Natraj."

Everyone was happy when I came out of my Yoganidra. I had told my mother how Shiva brought me out from that dormant state.

Once more, I had reached the ashram of sage Dadhichi. He gave me a rudraksha. It turned out to be the one that I had floated down the river.

Handing that over to me, he had said, "Sati, one day it's going to take you to Shiva."

"I'll keep it near my heart, sir," I whispered.

Then, he ordered me to touch a Shivalinga. Following his instruction when I touched it, a shudder had run down my body.

At that instant I had felt that no power in the universe could create any rift between Shiva and me.

Overcome by pride, my father would insult anyone. His chronic antipathy for Shiva was a source of great suffering for me. Then one day, he had announced before others my swayamwar.

"What are you going to do now, Sati?" Khyati didi had asked me.

Even mother had told me, "Sati, now I've begun appreciating the superb qualities of Shiva! Will he come here and help you out from this complex problem?"

"What makes you doubt it, mother?"

"Your father will never invite Shiva is my view!"

"But he's sure to come here," I said calmly.

A greater drama was to take place in my swayamwar. My father was determined that in case Shiva should get an entry into the event. Fearing that Shiva could reach there in disguise, he had a mirror made up that exposed the false entry of anyone. All were filled with doubts. Even I was stricken with incertitude. I remember how my father had tried in every way to have that Shivaling broken up into pieces that I was so fond of. It was precious to me more than my own life. But, notwithstanding all those uncertainties, I was not under any mental pressure.

The durbar hall of Prajapati Daksha was the most beautiful thing. Its majesty was unparalleled in every way. Its décor was the most exotic one. Its opulence impressed all those present there. It had expansive artistic casements. Studded with precious gems, they sparkled when light fell upon them.

It was a big gathering of exceptional and accomplished would be grooms. It comprised gods, gandharvas and renowned beings. At the very entrance, my father had kept a stone statue of Shiva as a janitor. Everything was going on smoothly.

They brought me to the hall. I had a big and beautiful garland of flowers in my hand. It was to be put round the neck of one of them.

My father then told me, "Sati, all these rare persons have come here with a wish to be chosen as your life partner. You can choose any one of these."

I looked around. On seeing the statue of my dear one as a janitor at the entrance of the hall, I could understand his subtlest leela. Even from that distance, I could feel the warmth wafting from that statue and seeping into my being. What seemed to be a stone statue to there was a different thing for me. I could even hear its throb through that din.

My face had brightened up. Standing before that statue, I stood still for some time. I felt, it was just looking at me. All present there were confused by my gestures and movements. Some of them wondered at my conduct. But there were some others who could perceive clearly the trend of the future events.

My father spoke up in a loud voice, "Sati, why have you been frittering away your time by standing before the stone statue of that kapali, aughad Shiva." A strange smile came over his lips as if he was very happy over his victory against Shiva. My face was blank when he uttered again, "Today, I've finally defeated my sworn enemy that aughad Shiva. I must celebrate now my ultimate victory over evil. He'll never get on my nerves again!"

I then spoke up, "Shiva, my dear love, now come before us and marry your Sati." I paused. A profound silence had spread over the place. All eyes were then focused upon me only. Breaking that prolonged silence, I pleaded, "Shiva, save your eternal beloved from indignity and disgrace today. Today your primordial energy–Adi Shakti– gives you the order."

There was a loud explosion and my dear Lord had lowered his head. I put that garland round his neck. The resounding sound of his damru echoed through the whole city. Daksha Nagri – the city of Daksha – was filled with the loud utterances of 'Har-har Mahadeva' from all corners of the place. Even the sage Dadhichi had reached there with his disciples. They had all been uttering and chanting the name of Shiva loudly and, were exultant with the completion of the event.

All those present there were very happy. They had begun congratulating my father. But his face had dulled.

"I don't give my approval to this marriage," he announced in a loud voice.

My grandfather had tried to reason out with him. He refused to accept the advice of his father, Brahmadeva. He was so adamantine that all protests and mentoring failed against his obduracy. At the end when Narayan appeared at the scene and ordered my father to approve the marriage, then, reluctantly he had to accept the alliance.

It was a cosmic event of the union of Shakti and Shiva.

My father's heart was filled with rancor. He had never concealed his own abhorrence for Shiva. Notwithstanding my mother's advice, he had expressed his inner thoughts before all. He could never rise about his umbrage. Maybe, it was some psychological problem. The venom of jealousy and anger kept suppurating in his system.

While sending me away, he said to me, "Sati, today you've let down your father before all. You've torn apart his dignity in the most feelingless manner. A time will come when your own dignity will be rent in the very same way."

He had cursed me loudly before that huge gathering. The going away from my father's place was a very painful event. The others could never fathom my agony. It had marred my happiness.

❑

My contact with Shiva brought about a complete change in my psyche. His simplicity accounted for his infinite charm. Living with him sharpened my vision. He had a great insight into all systems of the cosmos. He was an excellent psychologist. So, he could see through my silent suffering, and he tried to console me in his own style. My frozen grief thawed in the warmth of his company.

"Don't let these unpleasant circumstances upset you in any way, Sati. Try to undo the knot inside you," he told me one day.

"I'm happy here," I mumbled.

"You mustn't conceal anything from me," he said sentimentally.

Flashing a smile at him, I said, "My world now revolves around you."

"It makes me confident," he said rather vaguely. "Don't let the past haunt you in any way. I know you're pained by your father's words," he observed sympathetically.

I then told him, "Don't worry about me at all now, Shiva. I've recovered completely now. I know when one's time is unfavorable, all relationships become uncertain. Even snap off some time.

He took my hands into his. Then, he said, "Sati, even situations keep changing constantly as our own views and philosophies.

Then, I said, my face glowing with a feeling of camaraderie, "I only wanted you in my life. Now, you've come into my life and, I've been freed from all entanglements."

Shiva then observed, "Prajapati Daksha is very obdurate. His doors have been closed on you forever. I feel one should put in all his efforts in undoing the knot in his or her relationship. Only a knot free thread can pass through the eye of a needle. And, this is a complex task."

I told him, "Our relationship is going to last for a long time to come."

He had some presentiment. He said, slowly but, in a very clear tone, "A wait may last till eternity, Sati. Something we cannot fight against our destiny."

I had taken over the entire management of Kailash into my hand. I had disciplined the unruly associates and attendants of Shiva too. They were very happy with my presence. I experienced a profound peace in Kailash. The sense of closeness that I experienced at my new abode was not available to me in the midst of all luxuries of my father's palace. But there were some isolated moments when I would brood over my life with my family and be sad about that. But it would not last for a long time. I had a perfect identification with Shiva. I had got a new meaning of life at my husband's place. He had filled up a big void in my life. Not only that much, he was now completely absorbed in the pleasures of his own domesticity. In fact, husband and wife are a foil to each other.

We had often very serious discussion over different topics.

"Sati, dharma is the purest thing and above all faults. A man may go against humanity, but not the dharma."

"Have you been saying this thing in context of Prajapati Daksha?"

"No!"

"Then, who have you been referring to."

"This is born out of my own philosophy of life."

"Even, I want to say something."

"Yes?"

"Pay all attention to me."

"Yes-!"

"I've become a proud person now," I said.

"I don't think so."

"You're a victim of love. So, you have been overlooking the obvious."

"What has made you a proud person?"

I said, "I've won the love of the one whose love is sought by many," I said.

Shiva laughed. "Now, you'll only end up by making me a proud person," he said, casting a long, searching glance at me.

It was an infinite world. It was the abode of the supreme entity. Only after coming over to Kailash, I realized the truth that Shiva was the most romantic person and a great lover too.

"You're a master in deception," I told him one day.

"How do you say that, Sati?" he asked with an expansive smile.

"You aren't what you seem to be," I said, gazing at him with love.

"This isn't very clear to me," he said.

"You're an accomplished thespian," I said with conviction.

He burst out into laughter. It pleased me a lot. I always wanted to hear his laughter.

One day I sat down at the left side of Shiva. He was lost in his meditation. But he had become conscious of my presence.

"You can't be my vama, Sati! Don't sit at my left side."

"Why can't I sit here?" I asked with a tinge of anger. Fixing my gaze upon his face, I spoke up,"

After getting married to you, the right of sitting on your left comes to me naturally.

"No-still not!" he said.

"Why not?"

"You've to take three vows before me first!"

"What are they?"

He said, then, "You'll never lie to me. There should be absolute transparency between a wife and a husband."

"Okay-I won't tell a lie and what else?"

"You won't conceal anything from me!"

"Okay- I accept that too." I eyed him. "And what's the third one by the way?"

He then said, "My dear soul mate, in my phallic form, I'm the very plinth of all life forms. The young unmarried girls, longing for handsome, talented life partners, adore and worship my symbolic form." I tried to conjecture the import of his cryptic statement. He continued, "Never ever be jealous of their feelings and give them your blessings too."

"Even this vow I accept without any reservation," I said. "Okay- here I've accepted all these three vows. "So what else now?"

Then, smiling, said Shiva, "Come over to my left side here my true Vama!"

I was very happy on seeing how his face has brightened up like a full moon.

We would have occasional exchange of bantering between us.

"You've lost the game to me," one day I told him playfully.

"How have I lost the game?" he asked me.

With a wide smile on my face, I said, "There was once a time that you wouldn't even bother to cast a single glance at me. But, now...!"

"But nowwhat?"

"You keep looking at me all the time!"

"Yes-now I accept my defeat," he said sportingly.

I loved his generosity. Overcome by love, I said, "None can defeat you, my Lord. You're a born winner!"

"Should I tell you one thing, Sati?"

"You don't have to seek my permission," I said with all sincerity.

"What I want from you is that you should put everything to a test of logic."

"I also want to tell you something."

"Yes!"

"I don't want to make you angry at all," I said in low tone.

"What're you afraid of?"

"I don't know how to put it across to you."

"Sati!"

"Yes, my dear Lord!"

"You must remember those three vowsYou can't overlook them."

"Then, I must tell you!"

"You must."

"You're very stubborn!"

"Is that your impression about me?"

"Yes?"

"Don't you think it's some sort of bias?"

"No- it isn't", I said, insistent.

"What else?"

"You've a mercurial temper!" He cast a tender glance at me and began laughing." What are you laughing at?"

"I've been laughing at your evaluation."

"What's wrong about that?" Stopping briefly then, I said in a taunting voice, "Perhaps, your defeat has irked you!"

"I've already accepted my defeat! Why do you split hairs now?"

"Do you regret over your defeat?"

"I don't?"

"It's difficult for a man to accept his defeat!"

"Sati, marriage demands all sorts of compromises."

"What do you want to tell me now?"

He said, "There isn't any issue of any defeat or

victory between a husband or a wife. It means just love Big love and nothing else. It exists in a profound harmony between them."

"Go, should a husband accept his wife's superiority over him?"

"Why can't he? He should!"

I then said, "All men are victims of pride!"

"It's too farfetched," he said.

"A man takes a woman for granted and thinks her to be his maid, acting at his beck and call."

Then Shiva said, "In my view, for a better and truly meaningful life, men and women should work together." He paused looking at me closely." Defeat and victory are related to contests and wars! Love can never be a war between the opposite sexes.

Instantly, I realized that he had a real understanding of all the duties concerning marriage. He was an ideal husband.

❑

I remembered Swarchha. She was the wife of sage Dadhichi.

"How do you find this place, Sati?" she had asked me.

"I love it."

"Really?"

"Yes! Do you have any reason for your doubting it?"

"You don't have any luxuries here!"

"I don't miss them at all," I told her.

"I appreciate your healthy attitude towards life!"

"But, even then, comforts matter a lot in human life."

I answered, "Only for those who're engrossed in the gross materialism!"

"I'm just trying to assess the situation, Sati! Don't take it otherwise."

"Were you expecting it otherwise?"

"No- Not at all."

"Then why is that faint smile on your face?"

"There is a secret behind it!"

"What secret?" I asked, consumed by curiosity.

She said, "My husband looks up to you."

"I know that!"

"Do you know the actual reason?"

"I don't know and you?"

"I know it. My husband told me once."

"What has he told you. Tell me if it isn't any breach of trust."

"I'll tell you," said Swarchha.

"Tell me."

She cast an intense glance at me and, then began telling, "He feels that saga of Shiva and Sati's is love will continue till the end of this world."

I looked at her. I said, "My own heart confirms your statement."

Swarchha said, "Your birth on the earth is with a unique purpose mission of all divinities." I looked at her. She explained, "The son born out from the union of Shiva and you would dispel darkness around and protect the spirituality by killing all demons." She paused, brooding over something, "It's possible has pointed out the great sage."

I asked, concerned, "What do mean by is possible?"

"The sage sees some problem too."

"I request you to let on everything without any hesitation, "I said, my eyes pleading.

She then said, "This alliance between you two had to go through very tough times." She stopped to muse over something. Quietly I waited for her to say something. "The life of a woman is tough and complex, Sati. She has to take care of everyone's feelings all the time. The others even try to direct her love too. This is very disgusting in my opinion."

"Make it clear," I said to her.

She went on, "My husband has said, it's difficult to make out what destiny has in store for a person! He didn't explain it in detail. However, what I could make out from his words is that he was worried over your future, Sati."

"Do you hide anything from your husband?" I asked her.

"No, Sati! I think it's a highly condemnable thing."

"Shiva loves the sage."

Lost in her own musings, she mumbled, "I must tell you something else too."

"Do so," I said, curious.

"Be a true follower of your husband."

"I'm fully devoted to him."

Now, I want to ask something, Sati?"

"You can."

"Aren't you afraid of the terrible form of Shiva?"

"Do you want to know the truth," I said, laughing.

"Yes."

"You're very perceptive Swarchha," I said appreciatively.

On that she spoke out, "My husband has told me about your real identity." She paused and, then folding her hand, she pleaded to me, "I've been told about your real purpose. Only you give meaning to Shiva. I feel all females of the world .... Creation is an image of your primordial form. A man attains meaning through his wife only. A union between Shakti and Shiva gives motion to each and every particle here. O Goddess Supreme, you're the one who gives a unique and the most meaningful dimension to love. You alone are the source of our well-being."

Holding her hands, I said, "Today, you've explained most beautifully the role of a woman as a wife and, also as a divine force. May God make you the happiest, woman on earth!"

❑

"Sati, why is a wife called vama?" My Lord asked me one day.

I said, "Perhaps in his own pride, he feels that a woman has a lower rank status. That's why he gives her a mean place!"

"Nope! You aren't right on this point!"

You explain it to me then."

"Vama is meant to give her a higher status."

"How?"

"Our entire life-giving system is mainly on the left side Our heart and the arterial system without that, we can't even survive," he said pensively.

"It means, a woman is superior to a man?"

"She is."

Living with kapali, aughad Shiva helped me scale new heights.

Life went on.

Shiva my dear Rudra was an eternal experience revelation. He had now become a perfect family man. There were moments when I would comb his matted, thick locks and powdered his face despite his loud protests. But I knew that he enjoyed all those expressions of love. As an ideal husband, he was fully aware of all my needs.

Very few in the world know who Shiva is! He is an endless, timeless existence... reality. Nothing exists beyond him. Nothing exists before and after him. he contains everything. He alone is responsible for all life and death. All unions and separations exist in him to. He alone is the ultimate cause. He is the most handsome and the best in the world. He is the motion and he is the stasis.

There were moments when I would be very sad while brooding over my father's failure in understanding and appreciating the real character of my husband. In those moments Shiva tried to calm me down.

One day I overheard Shiva's conversation with Narad.

"My Lord when will the formidable demon Tadkkasur be killed?" he asked. He paused and thought over something. His voice expressed concern when he said, "Now, you're a family man and, you know it that the demon would only be killed by your son from the mother!"

Shiva's voice was serious when he said, "Narad, all will have to wait for some more time. I don't know what destiny wants from me."

On that Narad said, “My Lord, you’re the cause of everything. You’re the sole determiner of all happenings in the entire universe.”

Face serious, gravely said Shiva, “Narad, it’s true that I set up all rules and, yet I too am not free from their compulsion either. Right now, I don’t have any idea of the future course. But whatever it is, it’s hazy.

Kailash covered a vast area. Its natural beauty was enhanced by different kinds of objects. There were beautiful and colorful flowers and vegetation in galore. There were beautiful birds and land animals. Its verdure was something that appealed to a visitor instantly. The numerous crystalline streams and rivulets added further to its charm. Its cool breeze refreshed me. Every day I would go on my excursions to some unseen place. All the while Nandi accompanied me for my protection.

Then, one day I saw different goods and goddess and some others going in one direction.

“Where are they heading for, Nandi?” I asked.

“I don’t know, mother,” he said to me.

“Go there and find out,” I told him. “I’m serious about it!”

He had come back.

“Mother,” he said. Looking at me strongly, “your father, Prajapati has arranged a yagya at his place. All those are going to participate in it.”

I was happy. "I'll so there too with Shiva," I said with the utmost cheerfulness.

"Yes mother!" said Nandi, his face looking dull.

After coming back, I told Shiva excitedly, "Now be ready for festivities!"

"What festivities?" he asked, wondering.

"My father has arranged a big yagya and, we must be present there too," I said exultantly.

"Sati, we haven't been invited! How can we go there?"

He must have forgotten it!"

"This is unusual."

"All the same I'm his dearest daughter and we shouldn't fuss over a small thing!"

"I can't go uninvited!"

"You don't care for my feelings!"

"I advise you not to go there either. I've a strange premonition", said Shiva.

"My father loved me most! Even if he's angry after seeing me his anger will evaporate," I said emphatically. "I'm very sure about it."

"Sati!"

"Yes?"

"Don't go there!"

"I will."

I won't."

"Okay- then, I'll go there all alone."

He looked at me. I saw sadness in those eloquent eyes. "As you wish it, I'll bid good- bye to you then. Nandi will accompany you."

I had reached my father's place.

"Why have you come here?" my father asked me bluntly.

"Why, I'm your daughter," I could only say that much then.

"You were the one earlier. Now you aren't."

"Have you rejected me?"

"Yes?"

"You don't have any feelings towards me now?"

"That's the truth." He paused and stared at me. His eyes were full of anger and hatred. Then, tauntingly, he asked," And, where is your that kapali husband. I must congratulate you! At least you have come here without him. His filthy presence would have vitiated the atmosphere of this place!"

"Now don't say anything against your own son-in-law!"

"I don't accept him as the one. Neither are you my daughter nor is he my son-in-law. Do you get it?"

Annoyed greatly, I said," I can't put up with your utter nonsense any more Daksha."

He burst out, "You impudent and uncultured female, you have been using these insulting words against me at my own place." He stopped for some time. Then he said in an angry and venomous voice, "Your husband is the worst specimen in the world. I'll curse him a thousand times. His monstrosity makes me shrink back in abhorrence."

All others present there kept listening to us quietly.

"You're all here a bunch of cowardly people. Can you have any yagya with giving an offering to Shiva? I wonder why you have one listening so passively to the words of irreverent Daksha. Don't you see that he has gone mad?"

Daksha burst out, "Here, you leave my place immediately. Go back to that filthy Shiva and perform your wifely duties! You're a bête noire in this sophisticated society. Your life partner too is a two-penny thinker. He is a practitioner of the black-magic. His very presence at a place is a bad omen. I've no doubts that he indulges freely in omophagy! He makes a system fall apart and causes the worst mayhem to the innocent people."

"Stop it now, Daksha!" I hissed angrily. All of them looked frightened." You're a conceited and overweening person. I regret that I've been related to you in any way. "I paused and panted. I began," No longer am I going to live in this body that is identified with you. I'll destroy it."

Laughing mordantly, Daksha said, "Even I don't want to be identified with you and your sinister sorcerer. You can do anything to your own body. Here, I want to tell you one more thing." I cast a searing glance at him." Sati, you stink! You foulmouthed female, your vain recalcitrance can't affect and mar the dignity of great Prajapati." He paused before he said, "As you back up the evil, you're an evil too!"

I roared with passion. I muttered, "My dear Shiva, forgive your foolish wife. I went against your wishes and now, I can't get back to you with this body of mine. I must destroy it. I can't offer it to your any more. Its sanctity is lost in this polluting place of foolish Daksha!"

Grandfather Brahmdeva said, his voice full of suffering, "You idiot Daksha! Stop the imminent destruction! You could never understand why my head was cut off." Then, turning towards me, he said in his softest voice," Sati, my granddaughter, you condone the sin of your idiotic father! He has put aside all courtesy and good manners!"

His words had further incensed Prajapati. Angrily, he said, "I just don't care about anything. Brahamadeva, only you fawn before that kapali Shiva. But, never forget that I don't."

I called in my yoga fire and surrendered my body to it. It was produced within me and existed in me only. Before losing my consciousness, I could hear the others crying and talking among themselves.

Grandpa's words floated into my ears, "You foolish and ignorant Daksha, you never deserved to be a Prajapati. You aren't even aware of the harm you've done to all!"

Gradually, coolness settled over me.

❑

Epilogue

As soon as the news of Sati's self-immolation reached Shiva, he sent the formidable Virbhadra, the extended image of his own self, to destroy Daksha. Prajapati Daksha then appealed to all for saving him from the wrath of Virbhadra. But none present these had the power and courage to oppose the unconquerable might of Shiva.

Virbhadra destroyed the yagya of Daksha and eliminated all those who came on his way. He cut off the head of Daksha. Those present there had begun crying for mercy. Daksha's wife and daughters had begun mourning bitterly. Prasuti began beating her chest in grief.

Virbhadra's roar echoed through the place and frightened all those present there. That yagyasala and palace had now been turned into a graveyard. All gods, sages and other spiritual luminaries had begun imploring in unison to Shiva to bring Daksha back to life.

They said, O Supreme Being, we supplicate to you. It is necessary for the management of the world

Creation. Moreover, at the last moments of his life, Daksha had sought your mercy. The death from your pious hands has exculpated him from his sins."

On their pleas, Shiva placed the head of a goat on Prajapati's neck and brought him back to life.

"Now, the whole universe will have to wait for eons before they're protected and saved from the cruelties of the demon Tadkasur," said Lord Vishnu, looking at those present there.

With that goat-head, Daksha sought the forgiveness of Shiva.

Placing Sati's body over his shoulder, Shiva had gone away from there.

In those moments it seemed as if the entire Creation had come to a standstill. A vast and impenetrable silence had swallowed down everything.

❑